A Treasury for
CAT
LOVERS

Wit and Wisdom, Information and Inspiration
About Our Feline Friends

RICHARD LEDERER
Bestselling Author of *Anguished English*

HOWARD BOOKS
A DIVISION OF SIMON & SCHUSTER, INC.
New York • Nashville • London • Toronto • Sydney

Illustrated by Jim McLean

Our purpose at Howard Books is to:
Increase faith in the hearts of growing Christians
Inspire holiness in the lives of believers
Instill hope in the hearts of struggling people everywhere
   Because He's coming again!

 Published by Howard Books, a division of Simon & Schuster, Inc.
1230 Avenue of the Americas, New York, NY 10020
www.howardpublishing.com

ISBN 978-1-4767-3816-1
10 9 8 7 6 5 4 3 2 1

Manufactured in the United States of America

For information regarding special discounts for bulk purchases, please contact: Simon & Schuster Special Sales at 1-866-506-1949 or business@simonandschuster.com.

The Simon & Schuster Speakers Bureau can bring authors to your live event. For more information or to book an event, contact the Simon & Schuster Speakers Bureau at 1-866-248-3049 or visit our website at www.simonspeakers.com.

Edited by Chrys Howard
Cover and interior design by Stephanie D. Walker
Illustrations by James McLean

To Little and Big,
Twinkie and Normal,
Victoria and Albert,
Fur Fur,
Max and Lizzie,
and all the other cats who have owned me

Acknowledgments

The verb *to vet* means "to examine credentials, manuscript, or other documents as a veterinarian examines an animal, hoping to give it a clean bill of health." I thank the senior staff of the San Diego Humane Society for vetting the text of this treasury to ensure that the facts are accurate and the tone sensitive.

I also thank Bob Vetere, of the American Pet Products Association, for vetting the statistics in the Introduction.

I have striven mightily to track down the source of every item in this book that isn't of my own making. To those creators whom I have not been able to identify, I hope you are pleased that your luminous contributions gleam, albeit anonymously, from these pages.

Contents

Introduction: Wholly Cats!

A meow massages the heart.
—Stuart McMillan

**Who could believe such pleasure
from a wee ball o' fur?**
—Irish Saying

Two women were conversing in a supermarket aisle:

"Horace and I have been together ten years now, and he makes me very happy," one said, "so I don't mind buying him what he likes even if it is more expensive."

"Well, with my Benny I have no choice. He's just plain fussy," her friend replied.

Both women were loading their shopping carts with high-quality cat food.

In ancient Egypt, cats were worshiped as gods, and cats have never forgotten that. Back then, killing a sacred cat was punishable by death. When the family cat died, the entire family would shave off their eyebrows as a sign of mourning. In their cats' burial sites, Egyptians would place embalmed mice as afterlife snacks.

Cats have had their ups and downs. In the Middle Ages, the pagan associations of cats caused them to become outcasts. They were labeled evil creatures.

Today cats have made a spectacular comeback. The cat, not the dog, is now the most popular pet in our nation. Approximately ninety million

Feline Americans reside here, compared to seventy-seven million Canine Americans, and—a distant third—fourteen million Parakeet Americans. More than one in three U.S. families (34 percent) are graced by a cat, a higher proportion of households than include children.

Our mass ailurophilia (love of cats) speaks volumes about America. "The greatness of a nation and its moral progress," said Mahatma Gandhi, "can be measured by the way its animals are treated." Americans fork out more than forty-three billion dollars on their pets each year, spending eight billion dollars on dog food and four billion dollars on cat food, more than on baby food. An estimated one million cats in America have been named as primary beneficiaries in their owners' wills.

Such devotion should come as no surprise. Human beings are fascinated and beguiled by the mysterious aloofness of cats; their swift prowess as hunters; their sensuous, sculpted bodies; their elegant, acrobatic grace and agility; their kittenish curiosity and mischief; and their regal dignity. Our lives with cats are not only ennobled, they are made longer: studies show that owning a cat alleviates loneliness, anxiety, and depression; reduces stress, high blood pressure, and heart disease; and adds six months to the average person's life.

For us cat lovers (ailurophiles, if you prefer a fancy word for that tribe), magical, mystical cats are a blessing to life. They . . .

- warm our laps and our hearts;

- give us someone to talk to and to spoil;

- create a bond with other cat people;

- turn common household objects into cat toys;

- donate their services as alarm clocks;
- are living adornments of our homes;
- keep mice on the run;
- remind us that there are still wild things in our world;
- remind us that life is mysterious;
- inspire poets, writers, moviemakers, creators of musical theater, artists, and cartoonists;
- and hold the purr strings to our hearts.

So the least we lucky cat lovers can do is write a book in praise of our feline friends. This is that book.

Richard Lederer
San Diego, California
richard.lederer@pobox.com

1 Are You a Cat Lover?

Cats are love on four legs.
—*Richard Torrergossa*

One small cat changes coming
home to an empty house
to coming home.
—*Pam Brown*

Let's start from scratch. Cat lovers have a special attraction to those purring lapfuls of fur who sometimes deign to cohabit with them. Cat people are a special breed not recognized by the Cat Fanciers' Association. You know you're a cat lover if . . .

- You can't go more than a half hour without craving to pat a furry head.

- There is no sweeter sound to your ears than a feline purring.

- All of your clothes have cat hair on them, even when they come back from the Laundromat or dry cleaner. Cat hair is everywhere—on your rug, your bedspread, your packing tape, and in your sinks. When you find a cat hair in your food, you remove it and blithely go on eating.

- Lint rollers are on your shopping list every week.

- Your floors are littered with cat toys.

- You have no small children at home, but you refer to yourself as "Mommy" or "Daddy."

- Your parents refer to your pet as their grandcat.

- You often talk in a goofy high voice.

- The rolls of toilet paper in your bathrooms are partially shredded.

- Your vet's receptionist recognizes your voice. That's because when you and your cat get sick, you take the cat to the vet's but settle for an over-the-counter remedy for you.

- The instructions to the cat kennel are longer than the instructions to the house sitter.

- You get birthday cards for your cat from family, friends, and the vet. When you send them cards, you sign for your cat.

- You keep a mental list of people you would like to spay or neuter. You like people who like your cat and despise people who don't.

- You sleep in the same position all night because it annoys your cat when you move.

- You put off making the bed until the kitty wakes up.

- You absentmindedly pat people on the head or scratch them behind their ears.

- You cringe at the rising price of food in the grocery store but think nothing of the cost of cat food or treats.

- You carry cat treats in your pocket or purse at all times.

- You have more than four opened but rejected cans of cat food in the refrigerator.

- You watch bad TV because your cat is sleeping on the remote.

- You spend more time shopping at the pet store than you do at the clothes store.

- You think nothing of spending five-hundred dollars on gas, two-hundred dollars on a motel room, and one-hundred-fifty dollars for meals to bring home a thirty-five-cent prize ribbon.

- In your photo album, there is scarcely a picture of anybody with two legs.

- Your cat is the star of your Web site.

- *Garfield* is your favorite comic strip and *Tom* and *Jerry* your favorite movie short subject.

- Your cat's name is featured on your license plate or license-plate holder.

- You love bringing home cat bags. You never completely finish a piece of chicken or fish so your cat gets a taste, too.

- You leave the sock drawer open so your cat can sleep in it.

- You stand at an open door indefinitely in the freezing rain while your cat sniffs the door, deciding whether to go out or come in.

- The first question you ask when on a date is: "So, do you like cats?"

- Every chance you get, you lecture people on responsible cat ownership.

- You type using no capital letters because there's a cat on your arm preventing you from using the shift key.

- You believe that every life should have nine cats.

- When you leave home, you pat your spouse on the head and kiss your cat goodbye.

- If you're an author, you dedicate your books to your cats (as I have).

Fascinating Feline Facts 2

Thou art the Great Cat,
the Avenger of the Gods,
and the Judge of Words,
and the President of
the Sovereign Chiefs,
and the Governor
of the Holy Circle.
Thou art indeed the Great Cat.
—*Inscription on the Royal Tomb at Thebes*

- All cats are members of the family *felidae*. The cat family split from the other mammals at least forty million years ago, making them one of the oldest mammalian families. Today's house cats are descended from wildcats in Africa and Europe. Domesticated over 3,500 years ago, cats have been part of every civilized human society.

- In 1758 Swedish naturalist Carolus Linnaeus classified the domestic cat as *felis catus*. Cats are also identified as *felis domesticus*.

- The Egyptian goddess of fertility, Bast, was often represented as a cat. Ra, the Egyptian god of the sun, changed himself into a cat to battle the serpentine darkness.

- No domestic cats reside in the Chinese zodiac. According to legend, the Jade Emperor called the animals to him, promising to name a year for those who most promptly appeared. The rat tricked the cat, who arrived too late, and ever since the two beasts have been enemies.

- A group of adult cats is called a clowder. A group of kittens is called a kindle.

- In general, cats live longer than dogs. The typical life span is twelve to fourteen years. On average, indoor cats live five years longer than outdoor cats, who are at risk for being run over, killed by predators, and being subjected to extremes of weather. Some cats' lives reach beyond twenty. The oldest known cat was Ma, a female from Devon, England, who was thirty-four when she died in 1957.

- Cats usually range from about three to eighteen pounds. According to the *Guinness Book of World Records*, Snowbie, a cat born in Aberdeen, Scotland, in 1993, weighed forty-eight pounds. A Maine coon cat named Verismo Leonetti Reserve Red, "Leo" for short, measured forty-eight inches from the tip of his nose to the tip of his tail. Leo was born in Chicago in 2002.

- "To err is human, to purr feline," quips Robert Byrne. Kittens begin purring when they are one week old. A cat purrs at about twenty-six cycles per second, the same frequency as an idling diesel engine. Purring is part of every cat's repertoire of social communication, apparently created by the movement of air in spasms through contractions of the diaphragm. Small cats, such as our domestic species, purr with each outward and inward breath while big cats, such as lions and tigers, generate their sounds only when exhaling. So big cats, with the exception of cheetahs and bobcats, don't really purr, but small cats don't really roar.

- A cat almost never meows at another cat. Cats use this sound for humans. Cats possess more than one hundred vocal sounds, while dogs have about ten.

- After cats eat, they always immediately bathe themselves. This is because their instinct tells them to get the food scent off of them so that predators will not smell the food and come after them.

- A cat will clean itself with paw and tongue after a dangerous experience or when it has fought with another cat. This is believed to be an attempt by the animal to soothe its nerves by doing something natural and instinctive.

- Touching noses helps a kitten relate to its mother. Throughout a cat's life nose touching remains a friendly method of greeting humans and other cats.

- A female cat can begin mating when she is between five and nine months old, a male between seven and ten months. If left to her own devices, a female cat could, in theory, give birth to seven kittens every four months. A Texas tabby named Dusty gave birth to 420 kittens. This is why population control using spaying and neutering is so important. In general, these procedures extend a cat's life by two to three years.

- In cats, the calico and tortoiseshell coats are sex-linked traits. Almost all cats displaying these coats are female, with a small occurrence of sterile males.

- Catnip excites cats because it contains a chemical that resembles an excretion of the dominant female's urine. About a quarter of cats are unaffected by catnip, but the product can affect lions and tiger, as well as cats.

- In 1947 Ed Lowe invented cat litter, allowing many felines to come indoors as house pets. The brand name Kitty Litter was a registered trademark. Interestingly, tigers can be trained to use litter boxes—large litter boxes.

• The only domestic animal not mentioned in the Bible is the cat.

• Cats and dogs turn in circles before lying down because in the wild this instinctive action turns long grass into a bed.

• When you find your cat glued to the window intently watching a bird, making a strange chattering noise, and clicking his or her jaws oddly, your cat is merely acting on instinct. What your cat is doing is directly related to the killing bite that all cats, both domestic and wild, use to dispatch their prey.

• The blood type of most cats is A. Some are type B and AB.

• Male cats used to be called "ram cats." In a popular book titled *The Life and Adventures of a Cat* (1760), the main character was named "Tom the Cat." Ever since, male felines have been known as "tomcats."

• Never, ever feed your cats chocolate. Chocolate contains theobromine, an alkaloid that can cause a cat's arteries to constrict, heart rate to increase, and central nervous system to shut down.

All animals, except man,
know that the principal business of life is to enjoy it.
—*Samuel Butler*

- Live for the moment.
- Notice squirrels, investigate shadows, and chase butterflies.
- Make your own hours.
- Obey your instincts.
- Shred all documents.
- Test limits. Try new things.
- Claw your way to the top. That's what drapes are for.
- Get to know people and things in high places.

- Be willing to take leaps of faith.
- When life knocks you for a loop, land on your feet, lick your wounds, and move on. Take a moment to recover your dignity, but don't dwell on the past.
- Don't cry over spilt milk. Lap it all up.
- Stare unabashedly.
- Sneeze unabashedly.
- Stretch unabashedly.
- Be tolerant, but not overly accommodating.
- Be finicky. They'll try harder to please you.
- Project confidence in a mad world.
- Variety is the spice of life. One day, ignore people; the next day, annoy them.
- Realize that sometimes you can't explain your actions.
- Recycle: Share your victories. Always give generously. A small bird or rodent on the bed tells them you care.
- Make the world your playground.
- Exercise daily.
- Get plenty of sleep.
- Go barefoot.
- Keep clean.
- Know all the sunny places.

- On hot days, drink lots of water and lie under a shady tree.
- Claim your own chair.
- Flaunt your hair loss.
- Life is hard; then you nap.
- Don't stress out over your first gray whisker.
- Don't let anything or anyone put you out. That's your decision.
- Curiosity never killed anything, except maybe a few hours.
- It never does any harm to ask for what you want.
- Make your mark on the world.
- Let sleeping dogs lie.
- Own nothing and be owned by nothing.
- Meow and the world meows with you. Hiss and you hiss alone.
- Self-esteem is good. Being placed on a pedestal is not just a privilege. It's a right.

4 The Body Electric

The smallest feline
is a masterpiece.
—*Leonardo da Vinci*

A cat sleeps fat,
yet walks thin.
—*Fred Schwab*

- A cat uses more than five hundred muscles to leap, jump, and sprint. A cat is capable of sprinting thirty-one miles per hour, slightly faster than a human being, and can jump as much as seven times its height.

- A cat's body comes with 230 bones. A human body comes with 206. Ten percent of a cat's bones are found in its tail. The tail is a mirror of a cat's mind. A tail held high means happiness, a twitching tail is a warning sign, and a tail tucked in close to the body is a sure sign of insecurity. The domestic cat is the only cat species able to hold its tail vertically while walking. All wild cats hold their tails horizontally or tucked between their legs while walking. The feline tail also plays a vital part in the cat's balance and in the "righting reflex" that allows it to land on its feet after falling from a height.

- A cat's brain is closer to a human's brain than is the brain of a dog. Both humans and cats have identical regions in the brain responsible for emotion. These similarities may be why we view cats as part of the family. Almost all cat owners admit they talk to their cats. That's good, because cats love to hear their humans' voices and the sound of their own name. So please talk to your cat often.

- Cats' eyes are the largest in proportion to their bodies of any mammal. The glow of a cat's eyes in the dark is usually greenish or golden, but the eyes of a Siamese reflect a luminous ruby red. You can tell a cat's mood by looking into its eyes. A frightened or excited cat will have large, round pupils. An angry cat will have narrow pupils. The pupil size is related as much to the cat's emotions as to the degree of light. Those dark lines connecting to a cat's eyes are called mascara lines. Cats watch more television than dogs do because cats are more visual and dogs more olfactory.

- The average cat possesses twenty-four whiskers, called *vibrissae,* twelve on each side of its nose, arranged in four rows. Each whisker is attached to two-hundred nerve endings that records air currents that the whisker senses. A cat uses its whiskers to determine if a space is too small to squeeze through. The whiskers act as feelers or antennae, helping the animal to judge the precise width of any passage. Never trim a cat's whiskers, as the animal will become disoriented in the dark.

- Cats lack a true collarbone and can generally squeeze their bodies through any space they can get their heads past. In the midst of building the Grand Coulee Dam in the state of Washington, engineers were stymied by the problem of threading a cable through a pipeline until an anonymous cat saved the day. Harnessed to the cable, this unknown hero crawled through the pipeline maze to successfully finish the job.

- Cats grow true fur, meaning that they have both an undercoat and an outer coat.

- An adult cat has thirty teeth. A cat's tongue is scratchy because it is lined with papillae—tiny elevated backward hooks that help to hold prey in place. To drink, a cat laps liquid from the underside of its tongue, rather than the top.

- A cat's arching back is part of a complex body-language system, usually associated with feeling threatened. The function of this display is to make the cat look as big as possible. The arch is able to get so high because the cat's spine contains nearly sixty vertebrae, which fit loosely together. Humans have but thirty-four vertebrae.

- According to tests made at the Institute for the Study of Animal Problems, in Washington, D.C., most dogs and cats, like people, are either right-handed or left-handed. That is, they favor either their right or left paws. Cats have carpal pads on their front paws that help to prevent them from sliding on a slippery surface when jumping. Like dogs, most cats have five toes on each front paw, but only four toes on each back paw.

- Cats are the only domestic animals who walk directly on their claws, not on their paws. This method of walking is called "digitigrade." When cats scratch furniture, it isn't an act of malice. They are actually tearing off the ragged edges of the sheaths of their old claws to expose the new sharp ones beneath. They are also marking territory with the multiple scent glands in the pads of their feet.

- A cat's heart beats at 110 to 140 beats per minute, about twice as fast as a human heart.

- A cat's jaws cannot move sideways.

- A cat's normal body temperature is 101.5 degrees F (38.6 C).

Uncommon Senses 5

The cat is nature's beauty.
—French Proverb

- A cat's daytime vision is only fair compared to a human's. But a cat sees more than six times better than a human at night because of the *tapetum lucidum*, a layer of extra reflecting cells that absorb light. Seeing far better than humans do at night and focusing best at a distance of eight to twenty feet make cats excellent nocturnal hunters. Cats can't see in total darkness, but in semidarkness their eyes pick up shards of moonlight and starlight to help locate their prey. Their peripheral vision is an astonishing 285 degrees, but a cat cannot see directly under its nose. This is why cats cannot seem to find tidbits on the floor.

- Cats have amazing hearing ability. A cat's ear has thirty muscles that control the outer ear. (By comparison, human ears have only six muscles.) Like a radar dish, these muscles rotate the ear 180 degrees, so the cat can hear in all directions without moving its head. A cat's hearing is one of the best in the animal kingdom. Cats can hear sounds as high-pitched as sixty-five kilohertz; a human's hearing stops at just twenty kilohertz. Young cats can distinguish between two identical sounds that are just eighteen inches apart at a distance of up to sixty feet.

- A cat's nose leather may be black or pink. Cats depend on their sense of smell for their very survival, and that sense of smell is fourteen times stronger than a human's. Blind at birth, kittens use their olfactory sense to locate their mother's source of milk. From then on, their olfactory acuity leads them to food, sometimes in the unlikeliest places, and helps them to find a mate and establish territorial boundaries. In addition to using their noses, cats can smell with the Jacobson's organ, which is located in the upper surface of the mouth. The so-called flehman response, in which cats curl back their upper lip, helps draw scent molecules back to Jacobson's organ.

- A cat's sense of taste is keener than a dog's. Cats use their sense of taste to determine which foods are good for them. As they are true carnivores, their sense of taste is programmed to identify protein and fat.

- The phenomenon of cats finding their owners in a place where they have never been before is scientifically known as psi-trailing. Many well-documented stories tell of cats who walked hundreds, even thousands of miles to find their owners. One such tale involved Ninja, who moved from Washington State to Utah in 1996. He disappeared shortly after the move, only to turn up at the old address a year later, having journeyed 850 miles. Like birds, cats have a homing ability that uses their biological clock, the angle of the sun, and the Earth's magnetic field.

The Cat's Got Our Tongue 6

There is no cat language.
Painful as it is for us to admit,
they don't need one!
—*Barbara Holland*

If cats could talk, they wouldn't.
—*Nan Porter*

The poet Carl Sandburg wrote, "The fog comes in on little cat feet." So does a large litter of our words and expressions. Whatever their ups and downs throughout history, cats have usually landed on their feet and have left their paw prints on our mother tongue.

Let's categorize the cats that run and leap and pounce and slink and purr and meow through our English language. I hope you'll find them to be, in the idiom of the Roaring Twenties, *the cat's meow, the cat's pajamas,* and *the cat's whiskers,* so called because the cat is capable of looking enormously pleased and satisfied.

Quick as a cat, let's make a "feline" for cat words in our English language.

The words *cat* and *pussy* derive from the Latin and Anglo Saxon names for the animal—*cattus* and *puus*. In some African languages, a man is referred to as a cat, which in American slang gives us the likes of *cool cat, hepcat*, and *fat cat*.

Cats have kittens, and so does our English language. *Kitty-cornered* issues from "cater-cornered," which comes from "quatre-cornered," which in French originally meant "four-cornered." By a process called folk etymology, speakers thought that in "quatre-cornered" they were hearing an analogy to a certain domestic feline. In the card game of faro the tiger was the bank or house, possibly because the tiger was once used on signs marking the entrance to Chinese gambling houses. Over the years gamblers transformed the tiger into a *kitty*, and it became the name for the pot in poker and other card games. Thus, when one contributes to the common store of betting money, one *sweetens* (or *fattens*) the *kitty*.

When the pussycat is absent (or taking a *catnap*), the mice have free run of the place, and *when the cat's away, the mice will play,* a proverb that reposes in many languages.

Cats, of course, have long been belled to prevent them from killing songbirds, but the expression to *bell the cat*, meaning "to take on a dangerous mission at great personal risk for the benefit of others," derives from the observation of a wise mouse. In one of Aesop's fables, the mice held a general council to consider what measures they could take to outwit their common enemy, the Cat. A young mouse stood up and said: "I propose that a small bell be procured, and attached by a ribbon around the neck of the Cat. By this means we should always know when the Cat is in the neighborhood." The proposal was met with general applause, until an old mouse rose and said, "That's all very well, but who will bell the cat?" The mice looked around at one another, and nobody spoke.

On the subject of cat-and-mouse games, we find a curious relationship between social history and phrase origins. Surprisingly, feminists arrested during the suffragette agitation in England in about 1913 inspired the first popular use of the expression *to play cat and mouse with*. When imprisoned, the suffragettes often went on hunger strikes, and the British Parliament retaliated by passing the Prisoners' Temporary Discharge for Ill-Health Act. The bill provided that hunger strikers be set free while fasting, but, when they recovered, they were liable for rearrest to complete their sentences. Critics compared the government's action to a big cat playing with a little mouse and dubbed the legislation "The Cat and Mouse Act," which entered common parlance as *to play cat and mouse with.*

Harking back to its larger and fiercer ancestors, many cats have a passion for chipmunks, field mice, birds, and other outdoor animals. They proudly deposit the corpses at their owners' doorsteps or behind and under furniture, a practice that gave rise, about 1920, to the expression *looking like something the cat dragged in.* While cats are valued for hunting pests, they do not always discriminate among their prey, and the cat that goes after its owner's prized pet bird may be in for a good scolding. *To look like the cat that ate the canary* originally meant to look guilty, but nowadays means to appear smug and self-satisfied.

It is both ironic and telling that an animal without the power of human speech has made such significant contributions to our language. There abound a number of explanations for *it's raining cats and dogs,* including the fact that felines and canines were closely associated with the rain and wind in northern mythology. In Odin days, dogs were often pictured as the attendants of Odin, the storm god, and cats were believed to cause storms. Another theory posits that during heavy rains in seventeenth-century England, some city streets became raging rivers of filth carrying many drowned cats and dogs. But the truth appears to be more mundane. Cats and dogs make a lot of noise when they fight (hence, "fighting like cats and dogs"), so they have become a metaphor for a noisy rain.

Why can't some animals keep secrets? Because pigs squeal, yaks yak, and someone always lets the cat out of the bag. Not long ago, city slickers had to beware of buying a pig in a poke (bag) from a farmer who wasn't in any way a country bumpkin. The animals inside such pokes were sometimes cats or kittens the canny country folk had substituted for suckling pigs. When the merchant opened the poke, he often *let the cat out of the bag,* revealing the crafty farmer's secret. When the cat ran off, the city bumpkin was *left holding the bag.*

When a cat is attacked by a dog or other animal, it aggressively arches its back, a response that suggested the phrase *to get one's back up* to describe humans aroused into anger. On the other paw, cats are often pictured as grinning. Charles Lutwidge Dodgson, best known to the world as Lewis Carroll, popularized the Cheshire Cat in his children-of-all-ages classic, *Alice's Adventures in Wonderland* (1865). The Cheshire Cat in the story gradually faded from Alice's view, its smile being the last part of the animal to vanish. *To grin like a Cheshire cat* goes back before Carroll, and the source could be Cheshire cheeses, which were at one time molded in the form of a cat. Another theory contends that the cat grins because the former palantine of Cheshire once had regal privileges in England, paying no taxes to the crown.

The phrase *having kittens* suggests a condition of severe anxiety. In bygone, more superstitious days, pregnant women who experienced long, painful labors were thought to be bewitched and about to give birth to a litter of felines.

An old British expression advised that "There's more than one way of killing a cat than choking it with cream." This implied that a method of doing something was rather foolish, since cats like cream and wouldn't be able to choke to death on it. But the saying changed to *There's more than one way to skin a cat* and gradually took on its present meaning—that there are more ways than one of accomplishing something.

Both the droopy *pussy willow* and the tall, reedlike *cattail* are so called for their resemblance to a cat's freely swinging tail. Because of that visual similarity and because it "scratched" the back like a cat, some black humorist coined the name *cat-o'-nine-tails* for the terrible whip. In addition, the first Egyptian scourges were made of thongs of cat hide.

Cats have long been regarded as tenacious of life because of their careful, suspicious nature and because they are supple animals that can survive long falls. The old English saying *A cat has nine lives* goes back well before the sixteenth century, and the nine "tails" of the whip being similar to the nine lives of a cat might have suggested the full name *cat-o'-nine tails*.

When we say or write *no room to swing a cat*, we are not referring to the animal but to the knotted cat-o'-nine-tails whip used to punish disobedient sailors. The scourge was too long to swing below deck, so punishment was always applied outdoors and left scars like those from a cat's scratch.

This shortening of the name of the whip to *cat* also explains the title of this chapter. The anticipation of a beating by the cruel cat-o'-nine-tails could paralyze a victim into silence. That's why *Has the cat got your tongue?* came to mean "Are you unable to speak?"

7 Find the Hidden Cats

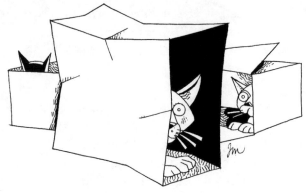

Cats assume their strangest,
most intriguing, and most beautiful postures
only when it is impossible to photograph them.
Cat calendars disappoint,
for they show only the public range of cat positions.
—*J. R. Coulson*

Now that we've let the cat words out of the bag, here are some statements about the felines hiding in our language. In some cases the cat in a word or expression meows clearly. In other cases a cat jumps out from a phrase and catches us by surprise. In a *caterpillar*, for example, hides "a hairy cat," from the Norman French word *catepelose*.

The clues that follow refer to a word or phrase that bears no relationship to the word *cat* beyond a mere coincidence of spelling. But each word or word grouping in the game you are about to play does begin with the letters *c-a-t*, and these letters are pronounced exactly like the name of the animal, as in "This cat throws rocks at castles: *catapult*":

1. This cat is a disaster. _____
2. This cat is a descriptive booklet. _____
3. This cat is a huge waterfall. _____
4. This cat tastes good on a hamburger. _____
5. This cat is classified. _____
6. This cat is cryptically buried underground. _____
7. This cat speeds a chemical reaction. _____
8. This cat chirps. _____
9. This cat swims. _____
10. This cat hopes one day to flutter by. _____
11. This cat is said to be in a lot of rackets. _____
12. This cat is a narrow bridge. _____
13. This cat is a set of religious questions and answers. _____
14. This cat is a whip. _____
15. This cat is a few winks out of forty. _____
16. This cat is a bunch of bull (and cow). _____
17. This cat is a marsh plant. _____
18. This cat is a game with string. _____
19. This cat walks on a diagonal line. _____
20. This cat is a sailboat. _____
21. This cat is a harsh cry. _____
22. This cat is a gem. _____

Chapter 7

23. This cat is a dupe, a tool of others. _____

24. This cat is a type of mental illness. _____

25. This cat is a place where one is "sitting pretty." _____

26. This cat shouts its disapproval. _____

27. This cat is x-ray-ted. _____

28. This cat is slang for "It's the greatest!" _____

Answers

1. catastrophe or cataclysm 2. catalog 3. cataract 4. catsup 5. category 6. catacomb 7. catalyst 8. catbird 9. catfish 10. caterpillar 11. catgut 12. catwalk 13. catechism 14. cat-o'-nine-tails 15. catnap 16. cattle 17. cattail 18. cat's cradle 19. catty corner 20. catamaran or catboat 21. caterwaul 22. cat's-eye 23. cat's-paw 24. catalepsy or catatonia 25. catbird seat 26. catcall 27. CAT scan 28. cat's meow, cat's pajamas, or cat's whiskers

The Creation of Cats 8

The cat was created when the lion sneezed.
—*Arab Proverb*

God made the cat in order that man
might have the pleasure of caressing the lion.
—*Fernand Méry*

On the first day of creation, God created the cat.

On the second day, God created man to serve the cat.

On the third day, God created all the animals of the earth to serve as potential food for the cat.

On the fourth day, God created honest toil so that man could labor for the good of the cat.

On the fifth day, God created the sparkle ball so that the cat might play with it, or might not play with it.

On the sixth day, God created veterinary science to keep the cat healthy and the man broke.

On the seventh day, God tried to rest, but He had to scoop the litter box.

Cat Genesis

When God created kitty cats,
He had no recipe;
He knew He wanted something sweet,
As sweet as sweet could be.
He started out with sugar,
Added just a trace of spice;
Then stirred in drops of morning dew,
To keep them fresh and nice.

He thought cats should be soft to pet,
So He gave them coats of fur.
So they could show they were content,
He taught them how to purr.
He made for them long tails to wave,
While strutting down the walk;
Then trained them in meow-ology,
So they could do cat talk.

He made them into acrobats,
And gave them grace and poise.
Their wide-eyed curiosity
He took from little boys.

He put whiskers on their faces,
Gave them tiny ears for caps,
Then shaped their little bodies,
To snugly fit on laps.

Made their eyes as big as saucers,
To look into man's soul,
Set a tolerance for mankind
As their purpose and their goal.
Benevolent and generous,
He made so many of them,
Then charged with fatherly concern
The human race to love them.

When one jumped up upon His lap,
God gently stroked its head.
The cat gave Him a kitty kiss,
"What wondrous love," God said.
God smiled at His accomplishment.
So proud of His selection.
He said, as He sat back, "At last,
"I've finally reached purr-fection!"

9 Our Sacred Pets

> Until one has loved an animal,
> a part of one's soul
> remains unawakened.
> —*Anatole France*

A Prayer for Animals
Hear our humble prayer,
O God, for our friends the animals,
especially for animals who are
suffering; for any who are hunted or
lost or deserted
or frightened or hungry; for all that
must be put to death.
We entreat for them all Thy mercy
and pity, and for those who deal
with them we ask a heart
of compassion and gentle hands
and kindly words.
Make us, ourselves, to be true
friends to animals and so to share
the blessings of the merciful.
—*Albert Schweitzer*

A Cat's Prayer (I)
Master, do not take me for a slave,
    for I have in me a taste for liberty.
Do not seek to divine my secrets,
    for I have in me a taste for mystery.

Do not constrain me with caresses,
>for I have in me a taste for modesty.

Do not humiliate me,
>for I have in me a taste for pride.

Do not abandon me,
>for I have in me a taste for fidelity.

Love me and I will love thee,
>for I have in me a taste for friendship.

A Cat's Prayer (II)

Beloved friend,

Although I am too proud to beg,

And may appear to be a very independent creature,

I ask for your loving care and attention.

I rely on you for my well-being much more than you
>may realize.

This I promise you, my benefactor, that I will not be a
>burden on you,

Nor will I demand more of you than you care to give.

I will be a quiet, peaceful island of serenity for you to
>gaze upon,

A soft soothing body to caress,

And I shall purr with pleasure to rest your weary ears.

Because I am a gourmet who appreciates different tastes,

I pray you will give me a variety of nutritious foods and
>fresh water daily.

Allow me, I pray, a warm sheltered place
Where I can rest peacefully and feel secure.

If I am wounded in battle or suffering from disease,
Please tend me gently, and see that I am tended
By loving and competent hands.

Please protect me from the inhuman humans
Who would hurt and torture me for their own
    amusement.
I am accustomed to your gentle touch and am not
    always suspicious
Nor swift enough to avoid such malicious acts.

In my later years when my senses fail me
And my infirmities become too great to bear,
Allow me the comfort and dignity that I desire for
    my closing days
And help me gently in my pain or passing.

Hear this prayer, dear friend. My fate depends on you.

A Cat's Prayer (III)

Now I lay me down to sleep,
On king-size bed, so soft and deep.
I sleep right in the center groove
My human pillow cannot move.

I've trapped her legs; she's tucked in tight,
And here is where I'll pass the night.
No one disturbs me, dares intrude
Till morning comes, and I want food.

I sneak up slowly to begin
My nibbles on my human's chin.
She bolts awake from my sharp teeth,
And soon my claws I will unsheathe.

Now I lay me down to sleep,
I pray this cushy life to keep.
I pray for toys that look like mice,
And sofa cushions, soft and nice.

I pray for gourmet kitty snacks
And someone nice to scratch my back,
For windowsills, all warm and bright,
For shadows to explore at night.

I pray I'll always stay real cool,
And keep the secret feline rule:
To never tell a human that
The world is really ruled by cats!

An Old Man's Prayer for His Cat

So many years ago she came to me, a trusting tiny ball of fluff who climbed up my leg to play and sleep upon my lap. All those years and still we share our joys and love; but now we both are grown old, and soon must die. Her eyes, like mine, are clouded and no longer serve to catch her prey. She would not understand the missing saucer, the cold hearth, and empty bed, nor bend her ways to suit some stranger's house.

Pray, take her first, O Lord, that I may see her resting safe beneath the apple tree that once she loved to climb with such agility, beyond my reach.

I shall grieve with understanding and then be ready to join my pet.

A Cat Owner's Prayer

Because I'm only human,
It's sometimes hard to be
The wise, all-knowing creature
That my cat expects of me.

And so I pray for special help
To somehow understand
The subtle implications
Of each proud meowed command.

Oh, let me not forget that chairs
Were put on earth to shred;
And what I like to call a lap
Is actually a bed.

I know it's really lots to ask
But please, oh please, take pity;
And though I'm only human,
Make me worthy of my kitty.

A Man and His Cat

A man and his cat were walking along a road. The man was enjoying the walk, when it suddenly occurred to him that he was dead. He remembered dying, and that his cat had been dead for years. He wondered where the road was leading them.

After a while, they came to a high, white stone wall along one side of the road. It looked like fine marble. The man and his cat walked toward the gate, and as he got closer, he saw a man at a desk to one side. When he was close enough, he called out, "Excuse me, where are we?"

"This is Heaven, sir," the man at the desk answered.

"Wow! Would you happen to have some water?" the man asked.

"Of course, sir. Come right in, and I'll have some ice water brought right up." The man gestured, and the gate began to open.

"May my friend come in, too?" the traveler asked, gesturing toward his cat.

"I'm sorry, sir, but we don't accept pets."

The man thought a moment and then turned back toward the road and continued the way he had been going.

After another long walk, and at the top of another long hill, he came to a dirt road that led through a farm gate that looked as if it had never been closed. There was no fence. As he approached the gate, he saw a man inside, leaning against a tree and reading a book.

"Excuse me," he called to the reader. "Do you have any water?"

"Sure, there's a pump over there." The man with the book pointed to a place that couldn't be seen from outside the gate. "Come on in."

"How about my friend here?" The traveler gestured to his cat.

"There should be a bowl by the pump."

They went through the gate, and sure enough, there was an old-fashioned hand pump with a bowl beside it. The traveler filled the bowl and took a long drink himself. Then he gave some to his cat. When they were full, he and the cat walked back toward the man, who was standing by the tree waiting for them.

"What do you call this place?" The traveler asked.

"This is Heaven," came the answer.

"Well, that's confusing," the traveler said. "The man down the road said that was Heaven, too."

"Oh, you mean the place with the gold street and gleaming gate? Nope, that's Hell."

"Doesn't it make you mad for them to use your name like that?"

"No. I can see how you might think so, but we're just happy that they screen out the folks who'd leave their best friends behind."

We are Siamese, if you please.
We are Siamese, if you don't please.
—*Walt Disney's* Lady and the Tramp

There are more than five hundred million domestic cats worldwide. More than seventy breeds are recognized by one cat registry or another, but the world's largest of these registries, The Cat Fanciers' Association, gives the nod to only forty.

Do I like all breeds of cats? Yes, Siamese-ily pleased. I own a long-hair Oriental cat. In fact, that's Himalayan over there. I couldn't find my cat for several days. I finally discovered him sleeping inside the dresser drawer. I guess you could say I went to the Bureau of Missing Persians. You see, I have no fear of long-haired cats: I'm not Angoraphobic. Some people say that the length of a cat's tail isn't important, but my friend Bobtails me it Manx a real difference in cats. When I put my cats out at night, I usually tell them, "Abyssinian you in the morning."

The word *pedigree* derives its pedigree from the Old French *pied de gru*, meaning "foot of the crane." Why? Because the clawlike, three-branched mark used in genealogical charts resembles the foot of the tall, leggy bird. Pedigree was first applied to human ancestry and later to the descent of cats, dogs, and other animals.

The first cat show took place in 1871 at the Crystal Palace in London. The event was the creation of writer, artist, and cat fancier Harrison Weir, who wrote: "I conceived the idea that it would be well to hold Cat Shows, so that different breeds, colours, markings, etc. might be more carefully attended to, and the domestic cat sitting in front of the fire, would then possess a beauty and an attractiveness to its owner, unobserved and unknown because uncultivated heretofore."

The most popular feline breed in America is the Siamese, which originated in Siam (modern-day Thailand). Legend has it that they were the companions of kings and priests and that they guarded temples. Some trace Siamese origins to Egypt and Burma, but many dispute this idea. Siamese were first brought to England in the late 1800s. Lucy Webb Hayes, wife of President Rutherford B. Hayes, is the first person recorded to own a Siamese cat in the United States. She named that cat Siam.

The color of the points in Siamese cats is heat related. Cool areas are darker. In fact, Siamese kittens are born white because of the heat inside the mother's uterus before birth. This heat keeps the kittens' hair from darkening on the points, which then show their duskier colors a few weeks after birth.

The Siamese is said to be the smartest of all cats. In reality, there is only one smartest cat in the world—and you own it!

Here are some intriguing facts about other breeds:

- In 2,000 B.C. an Abyssinian became the first domestic cat to appear in a painting. Abyssinians today still retain the jungle look of *felis lybica,* the African wildcat ancestor of all domestic cats. Abyssinians have "ticked" fur, with each hair displaying dark bands on a light background, in the manner of a hare.

- The Persian cat has the longest and thickest fur of all domestic cats, too long for self-grooming, The topcoat may be up to five inches long and the tail fur eight inches long.

- Manx cats get their name from the fact that they were originally bred on the Isle of Man. The Manx is a breed of cat with a naturally occurring mutation of the spine. This mutation shortens the tail, resulting in a range of tail lengths from normal to tailless. Many Manx have a small stub of a tail, but Manx cats are best known as being entirely tailless.

- California Spangled cats are a rare breed that resemble spotted wild cats. Most sell for $800 to $2,500, but in 1987 a California Spangled cat sold for $24,000.

- Ragdoll cats are so called because they are exceptionally docile in the hands of humans. Males weigh fifteen to twenty pounds and females ten to fifteen pounds, making the Ragdoll the largest of all feline breeds.

- The closest competitor to the Ragdoll in size is the Maine coon, which averages about fifteen pounds. Maine coon cats originated in Maine and got their name because, according to folklore, wild members of the species mated with raccoons.

- The Sphynx cat is a hairless breed that was recognized in 1966. Because they have no hair to keep them warm, Sphynxes prefer to nestle against other animals and people. They sometimes cuddle up and sleep with their owners under the covers.

- The Turkish Van, a very old and rare breed, is quite different from other cats because of its unusual love of water. Known as "the swimming cat," the Van is strong, quick, and agile. Vans are devoted and loyal companions—on land or in water.

The Difference between 11
Cats and Dogs

If you can look at a dog
and not feel vicarious
excitement
and affection,
you must be a cat.
—*Author Unknown*

Dogs lick you because they love you.
Cats lick you because you had chicken for dinner.
If a dog jumps up into your lap,
it is because he is fond of you;
but if a cat does the same thing,
it is because your lap is warmer.
—*Alfred North Whitehead*

I've been trying to train my cat to understand
the meaning of the word "no."
Which seems to be roughly equivalent
to teaching a dog Latin.
—*Judy Brown*

Women and cats will do as they please,
and men and dogs should relax and get used to the idea.
—*Robert A. Heinlein*

Cats are smarter than dogs.
You can't get eight cats to pull a sled through the snow.
—*Jeff Valdez*

Chapter 11

A dog is prose; a cat is a poem.
—*Jean Burden*

A dog is a man's best friend. A cat is a cat's best friend.
—*Robert J. Vogel*

If animals could speak, the dog would be a blundering,
outspoken, honest fellow,
but the cat would have the rare grace
of never saying a word too much.
—*Philip Gilbert Hamerton*

You can keep a dog, but it is the cat who keeps people,
because cats find humans useful domestic animals.
—*George Mikes*

A dog is a dog, a bird is a bird, and a cat is a person.
—*Mugsy Peabody*

You call to a dog and a dog will break its neck to get to you.
Dogs just want to please. Call to a cat and its attitude is
"What's in it for me?"
—*Lewis Grizzard*

A dog is like a liberal. He wants to please everybody.
A cat doesn't really need to know that everybody loves him.
—*William Kunstler*

The cat is a character of being; the dog is a character of doing.
—*Michael J. Rosen*

A cat is a demure animal;
it will not come into the living-room
wagging its tail and knocking over lamps and tables.
—*H. Monger Burdock*

Cats don't bark and act brave when they see something
small in fur and feathers.
Dogs tend to bravado. They're braggarts.
In the great evolutionary drama the dog is Sergeant Bilko,
the cat is Rambo.

—James Gorman

In order to keep a true perspective of one's importance,
everyone should have a dog that will worship him
and a cat that will ignore him.

—Dereke Bruce

To someone very good and just,
    Who has proved worthy of her trust,
The cat will sometimes condescend—
    The dog is everybody's friend.

—Oliver Herford

The humble dog don't ask for much—
    A praiseful word, a bone, and such.
He's grateful for the passing touch
    And loves those who bestow it.

The lofty cat struts, nose in air.
    You call; it answers with a stare,
Accepts, demands the finest care,
    Then acts as if you owe it.

—Benjamin Franklin Pierce

Dogs shed; cats shred. Dogs drool; cats rule.

A dog lives in your house and sees that you give it food and water and says to itself, "Wow, these beings give me food and water without my having to do anything. They must be gods!"

A cat lives in your house and sees that you give it food and water and says to itself, "Wow, these beings give me food and water without my having to do anything. I must be a god!"

A dog sees its master trapped on a roof and thinks, "Yikes! My master is in trouble!" A cat sees its master trapped on a roof and thinks, "Yikes! I don't know how to use a can opener!"

If you command your dog to "Come here," he runs right over with a "Yes, what can I do for you?" The cat's response is "Put it in writing, and I'll get back to you later." This is why dogs have masters, and cats have staff.

What Is a Dog?

- Dogs spend all day sprawled on the most comfortable piece of furniture in the house.

- They take up too much room in the bed.

- They can hear a package of food opening half a block away, but don't hear you when you're in the same room.

- They can look dumb and lovable all at the same time.

- They growl when they are not happy.

- When you want to play, they want to play.

- When you want to be alone, they want to play.

- They leave their toys everywhere.

- They do disgusting things with their mouths and then try to give you a kiss.
- They have an irrational fear of vacuum cleaners.
- They don't tell you what's bothering them.
- They mark their territory.
- They don't do dishes.
- They like to play dominance games.
- They don't notice when you get your hair cut.
- They do not understand what you see in cats.

  Conclusion: Dogs are furry little men.

What Is a Cat?

- Cats do what they want.
- They rarely listen to you.
- They are totally unpredictable.
- When you want to play, they want to be alone.
- When you want to be alone, they want to play.
- They expect you to cater to their every whim.
- They are moody.
- They leave hair everywhere.
- They are slinky.
- They purr when they are happy.

- They're finicky about their food.
- They scratch when they are angry
- They do not understand what you see in dogs.

  Conclusion: Cats are furry little women.

Why Cats Are Better Than Dogs

- Cats are way more independent than dogs. Cats are a perfect fit for a rising urban population and adapt easily to living in small spaces. They can tolerate being left alone for long periods of time as long as you provide water and a litter box. Many cats sleep the day away until you come home to feed and play with them.
- Cats eat less than dogs.
- Cats live longer than dogs.
- Cats have better memories than dogs. Tests conducted by the University of Michigan concluded that while a dog's memory lasts no more than five minutes, a cat's can last as long as sixteen hours, exceeding even that of monkeys and orangutans.
- Cats don't bark.
- Cats don't slobber up your face.
- Cats don't steal your underwear and parade it around the house.
- Cats don't view cat litter as a buffet.
- Cats don't demand that you play fetch with a ball.
- Cats don't snore as loudly as dogs.

Excerpts from a Dog's Diary

Day 1,054

8:00 AM—Woke up and stretched! *My favorite thing!*

8:30 AM—Dog food! *My favorite thing!*

9:30 AM—A car ride! *My favorite thing!*

9:40 AM—A walk in the park! *My favorite thing!*

10:30 AM—Got rubbed and petted! *My favorite thing!*

11:30 AM—Played with dog toys! *My favorite thing!*

12:00 Noon—Lunch! *My favorite thing!*

1:00 PM—The yard! *My favorite thing!*

2:30 PM—Eww. A bath. Bummer.

3:00 PM—Milk-Bones! *My favorite thing!*

4:00 PM—The kids! *My favorite thing!*

5:00 PM—Got to play ball! *My favorite thing!*

6:00 PM—Pooped in the yard! *My favorite thing!*

7:00 PM—Watched TV with the family! *My favorite thing!*

10:00 PM—Snack! *My favorite thing!*

10:30 PM—Slept on the bed! *My favorite thing!*

Chapter 12

Excerpts from a Cat's Diary

Day 1,054

My captors continue to taunt me with bizarre little dangling objects. They dine lavishly on fresh meat, while I am forced to eat dry nuggets. Although I make my contempt for the rations perfectly clear, I still must consume something to keep up my strength. The only thing that keeps me going is my hope of escape, and the mild satisfaction I get from destroying furniture. Tomorrow I may eat another houseplant.

Day 1,055

Today I was almost successful in my attempt to assassinate one of my captors by weaving around their feet while they were walking. I must try this at the top of the stairs. In an attempt to disgust and repulse these vile oppressors, I once again induced myself to throw up on their favorite chair. I must try this on their bed.

Day 1,056

Today I decapitated a mouse and brought them the headless body, in an attempt to make them aware of what I am capable of and to try to strike fear into their hearts. They only cooed and condescended about "what a good little hunter" I was. Hmmm. Not working according to plan.

Over time, I have come to see how sadistic they are. This afternoon, for no good reason, I was chosen for the water torture. This time it included a burning foamy chemical called "shampoo." What sick minds could invent such a liquid. My only consolation is the piece of thumb still stuck between my teeth.

Day 1,057

There was some sort of gathering of their accomplices. I was placed in solitary throughout the event. However, I could hear the noise and smell the foul odor of the glass tubes they call "beer." I overheard that my confinement was due to my power of "allergies." Must learn what this is and how to use it to my advantage.

I am convinced the other captives are flunkies and maybe snitches. The dog is routinely released and seems more than happy to return. He is obviously a half-wit. The bird, on the other hand, must be an informant, and speaks with them regularly. I am certain he reports my every move. My captors have arranged protective custody for him in an elevated metal cell. He is safe—for now.

13 A Cat's Guide to Humans

As every cat owner knows,
nobody owns a cat.
—*Ellen Perry Berkeley*

Cats are absolute individuals,
with their own ideas
about everything,
including the people they own.
—*John Dingman*

There are many intelligent species in the universe.
They are all owned by cats.
—*Author Unknown*

A human may go for a stroll with a cat; he has to walk a dog.
The cat leads the way, running ahead, tail high,
making sure you understand the arrangement.
If you should happen to get ahead,
the cat will never allow you to think it is following you.
It will stop and clean some hard-to-reach spot,
or investigate a suspicious movement in the grass;
you will find yourself waiting
and fidgeting like the lackey you are.
But this is not annoying to cat lovers,
who understand and appreciate a good joke,
even when it is on them.
—*Robert Stearns*

1. Introduction: Why Do We Need Humans?

So you've decided to get yourself a human being. In doing so, you've joined the millions of other cats who have acquired these strange and often frustrating creatures. There will be any number of times, during the course of your association with humans, when you will wonder why you have bothered to grace them with your presence. What's so great about humans, anyway? Why not just hang around with other cats?

Our greatest philosophers have struggled with this question for centuries, but the answer is actually rather simple: They Have Opposable Thumbs. This single attribute makes them the perfect tools for such tasks as opening doors, prying the lids off of cat food cans, changing television stations, and other activities that we, despite our other obvious advantages, find difficult to do ourselves. True, chimps, orangutans, and lemurs also have opposable thumbs, but they are nowhere as easy to train, and their incomes are limited.

2. How And When to Get Your Human's Attention

Humans often erroneously assume that there are other, more important activities than taking care of your immediate needs, such as conducting business, spending time with their families, or even sleeping. Although this is dreadfully inconvenient, you can make this work to your advantage by pestering your human at the moment it is the busiest. It is usually so flustered that it will do whatever you want it to do, just to get you out of its hair. Not coincidentally, human teenagers follow this same practice.

Here are some tried and trusted methods for getting your human to do what you want:

- Sitting on paper: An oldie but a goodie. If a human has paper in front of it, chances are good it's something they assume is more important than you. They will often offer you a snack to lure you away. Establish your supremacy over this wood pulp product at every opportunity. This practice also works well with computer keyboards, remote controls, car keys, and small children.

- Waking your human at odd hours: A cat's "golden time" is between three-thirty and four-thirty in the morning. Be sure to get enough sleep during the day so that you can be awake and fresh during these hours. If you paw at your human's sleeping face during this time, you have a better than even chance that it will get up and, in an incoherent haze, do exactly what you want. You may actually have to scratch deep sleepers to get their attention. Remember to vary the scratch site to keep the human from getting suspicious.

- When a human is holding up a newspaper to read it, be sure to jump at the back of the paper. They love surprises.

- Dart out quickly and as close as possible in front of the human, especially on stairs; when they have something in their arms; in the dark; and when they first get up in the morning. This will help their coordination skills.

3. Punishing Your Human Being

Sometimes, despite your best training efforts, your human will stubbornly resist bending to your whim. In these extreme circumstances, you may have to punish your human. Obvious punishments, such as scratching furniture or eating household plants, are likely to backfire. Being unsophisticated creatures, humans are likely to misinterpret these activities and then try to discipline *you*. Instead, we offer these subtle but nonetheless effective alternatives:

- Do not allow closed doors in any room. To get one open, stand on hind legs and hammer with forepaws. Once the door is opened for you, it is not necessary to use it. You can change your mind. When you have ordered an outside door opened, stand half in and half out and think about several things. This is particularly important during very cold weather or mosquito season.

- When your human is attempting to make the bed, hop on it and curl up in the center, or pounce on the sheet the human is trying to rearrange. If your human tries to ignore you by covering you with the sheets, move around and try to mess things up. Protest loudly when you're evicted.

- If you have to throw up, get into a chair quickly. If you cannot manage this in time, get to an Oriental rug. Shag is good, too.

- Stare impassively at your human while it is attempting a romantic interlude.

- Stand over an important piece of electronic equipment and feign a hair-ball attack.

- After your human has watched a particularly disturbing horror film, stand by the hall cupboard, and then slowly back away, hissing and yowling.

- While your human is sleeping, lie on its face.

- For ladies knitting, curl quietly into lap and pretend to doze. Then reach out and slap knitting needles sharply. This is what she calls a dropped stitch. She will try to distract you. Ignore it.

- For people doing homework, sit on the paper being worked on. After being removed for the second time, push anything movable off the table—pens, pencils, stamps—one at a time.

- Laundry presents many opportunities to hamper. Laundry fresh from the dryer is a perfect bed, since it is warm and soft. As soon as your human puts down the laundry for sorting, arrange yourself for a nap. If your human removes you, keep returning until the laundry isn't warm anymore. Now it's playtime. Pounce on anything your human tries to move around for folding, especially socks and nylons. For added fun, grab a sock and hide under the bed with it.

- Switch the labels on the cat food and the canned tuna. Your humans will love the zesty new taste of their casseroles.

- Whenever you do something wrong, try to make it look like the dog did it.

4. Activities for When Your Human Invites Guests into Your Home

- Determine quickly which guest hates cats. Sit on that lap during the evening.

- For guests who say, "I love kitties," be ready with aloof disdain, claws applied to stockings, or a quick nip on the ankles.

- Always use the cat box during an important formal dinner.

- Always accompany guests to the bathroom. For a while, just sit and stare. Then push open the bathroom door before they are done.

5. Rewarding Your Human: Should Your Gift Still Be Alive?

The cat world is divided over the etiquette of presenting humans with the thoughtful gift of a recently disemboweled animal. Some believe that humans prefer these gifts already dead, while others maintain that humans enjoy a slowly expiring cricket or rodent just as much as we do, given their jumpy and playful movements in picking the creatures up after they've been presented.

After much consideration of the human psyche, we recommend the following: cold-blooded animals—large insects, frogs, lizards, glow-worms, grass snakes, and the occasional earthworm—should be presented dead, while warm-blooded animals—birds, rodents, and your neighbor's Chihuahua—are better still living. When you see the expression on your human's face, you'll know it's worth it.

6. How Long Should You Keep Your Human?

Cats prefer not to own people. Cats would rather lease people, with an option. You are obliged to your human for only one of your lives. The other eight are up to you. Mixing and matching is recommended, though in the end, most humans (at least the ones that are worth living with) are pretty much the same. But what do you expect? They're humans, after all. Opposable thumbs will take you only so far.

7. Conclusion

Humans need to know basic rules. They can be trained if you start early, are consistent, and are always firm. You will then have a smooth-running household.

14 A Cat's Dictionary

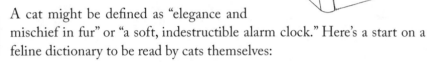

"Purrr.."

Cat: A pygmy lion who loves mice, hates dogs, and patronizes human beings.
—*Oliver Herford*

A cat might be defined as "elegance and mischief in fur" or "a soft, indestructible alarm clock." Here's a start on a feline dictionary to be read by cats themselves:

Aquarium. Interactive television for cats.

Can Opener. A device that unlocks the gates to purr-adise.

Catatonic. A feline's favorite soda.

Cat Bed. Any soft, clean surface, such as the white bedspread in the guest-room, the newly upholstered couch in the living room, or the dry cleaning that was just picked up. Also, a human lap.

Catnip. 1. A cat's bite. 2. The quicker picker upper.

Cat Owner. A cat who owns humans.

Catsup: Where a cat goes when a dog attacks.

Cat Toy. Anything not nailed down.

Children. Short humans of optimal petting height. Standing close to one assures you of some great petting. When running, they are good to chase. If they fall down, they are comfortable to climb on.

Claws. Portable shredding devices for slashing furniture and climbing curtains.

Deafness. A malady that affects cats when their human wants them in and they want to stay out. Symptoms include staring blankly at the human, then running in the opposite direction or lying down.

Dinner Table. That which you should sit under during meal times in order to catch falling scraps and hence to do your part to keep the home clean.

Dog. A cat's fitness apparatus for running practice. Way more fun than a treadmill.

Hors d'oeuvres. Bats, birds, bugs, chipmunks, gerbils, hamsters, mice, squirrels, and the like that cats use to supplement their diets and share with humans.

Housebreaking. An activity that is very important to humans, so you should break as much of the house as possible.

Humans. Adoring servants who exist to serve you. Automatic door openers and can openers.

Kneading. Cats are the kneadiest of animals, and it's people they knead the most.

Litter Box. An enclosed desert that spells relief.

Love. A feeling of intense affection, given freely and without restriction. The best way you can show your love is to rub up against your human being and purr. If you're lucky, your human will love you in return.

Mice. Interactive cat toys.

Milk. A catatonic.

Paper Bags. Inside of these dwell the Bag Mice. They are very small and the same color as the bag, so they are hard to see, but you can easily hear the crinkling noises they make as they scurry around the bag. You should do anything, including shredding the bag, to kill Bag Mice.

Purring. 1. The running of a well-tuned feline motor. 2. The sound of a cat manufacturing cuteness.

Scratching Post. Any vertical object in the house on which you can self manicure.

Sofa. An object that is to cats as napkins are to humans. After eating, it is polite to run up and down the front of the sofa and wipe your whiskers clean.

Tail. 1. A fifth leg used to maintain balance. 2. A portable hypnotic snake.

Tongue. A catty comb with flexible rubber bristles.

Tuna: A sonarlike device in cat food that causes cats to appear.

Vacuum Cleaner. Nature abhors a vacuum, and so do cats. You must flee from this roaring monster that tries to eat cats. When your human removes the swollen stomach from the inside of the vacuum cleaner monster, you must immediately pounce on and destroy that stomach.

Wastebasket. A cat toy filled with paper, envelopes, and old candy wrappers. When you get bored, turn over the basket and strew the contents all over the house to greet your humans when they come home. This is particularly fun to do when there are guests for dinner and you bat around the contents of that very special bathroom trash basket.

Whiskers. Feline radar useful for navigating through the labyrinth of life.

Yawn. A cat's honest opinion openly expressed.

Yummy. Anything on a human's plate.

There is, indeed,
no single quality in a cat
that a man
could not emulate
to his advantage.
—*Carl Van Vechten*

With the qualities of cleanliness, affection, patience, dignity,
and courage that cats have, how many of us, I ask you,
would be capable of becoming cats?
—*Fernand Méry*

Why a Cat Is Better Than a Woman

- A cat's parents never visit.

- A cat never expects you to telephone.

- A cat will not get mad at you if you forget its birthday.

- A cat never expects flowers on Valentine's Day.

- A cat does not care about the previous cats in your life.

- A cat does not get mad at you if you pet another cat.

- Cats don't care if you use their shampoo.

- Cats don't notice if you call them by another cat's name.

- If a cat is gorgeous, other cats don't hate it.

- Cats never need to examine the relationship.
- Cats understand that instincts are better than asking for directions.
- Cats don't hate their bodies.
- No cat ever put on a hundred pounds after reaching adulthood.
- Cats don't want to know about every other cat you ever had.
- Cats don't let magazine articles guide their lives.
- Cats never want foot rubs.
- Cats can't talk.
- Cats seldom outlive you.
- Cats don't shop.

Why a Cat Is Better Than a Man

- You can find a nice cat by advertising on a card in a shop window or in the classified section of the local paper.
- Cats miss you when you are gone.
- Cats don't brag about past relationships.
- Cats don't criticize your friends.
- Cats are very direct about wanting to go out.
- Cats are already in touch with their inner kittens.
- You can house-train a cat.
- Cats don't leave puddles on the bathroom floor.
- Cats will never touch the remote, don't care about football, and will cuddle up next to you as you watch romantic movies.

- Middle-aged cats don't feel the need to abandon you for a younger owner.
- Cats don't care whether or not you shave your legs.
- Cats don't feel threatened by female intelligence.
- You don't have to worry about who your cat is dreaming about.
- Good-looking cats don't know they are good looking.
- Cats don't want to bring their friends home for a beer.
- Cats don't tell the punch lines to your jokes.
- When cats beg, it's cute. When men beg, it's pathetic.
- Cats don't care if you have lipstick on when you kiss them.
- Cats don't mind morning breath.
- Cats love you without your morning shower and all the frou-frou stuff.
- Cats are satisfied with a belly rub.
- Cats don't complain about the amount of money you spend on clothes.
- You can neuter cats legally.
- Cats won't work your crossword in ink.
- Cats never answer your phone or borrow your car.
- Cats don't turn your bathroom into a library.
- Cats don't go through your medicine chest.
- Cats don't use your toothbrush, roll-on, or hair spray.
- With cats, the toilet seat is always the way you left it.
- Cats don't compare you to a centerfold.

- Cats will never call and say, "I have to work late, honey."
- Cats don't get embarrassed when you call them by a pet name when their friends are around.
- Cats don't have softball practice on the day you move.
- Cats don't care if you make more money than they do.
- Cats don't ask to be put through med school.
- There are fewer reasons to muzzle a cat in public.
- Cats have a highly developed sense of smell. Men, on the other hand, can quite happily wear the same pair of pants for a week.
- You'd feel guilty about turning a cat out on the street.

Why Cats Are Better Than Kids

- Cats eat less.
- Cats don't ask for money all the time.
- Cats are easier to train.
- Cats don't raid the refrigerator.
- Cats never ask to drive the car.
- Cats don't smoke, drink, or use drugs.
- Cats don't have to buy the latest fashions.
- Cats don't want to wear your clothes.
- Cats don't need a bazillion dollars for college.
- Cats can't see television images, so they don't grab the remote from you.

> The only mystery about the cat
> is why it ever decided
> to become a domestic animal.
> —*Sir Compton Mackenzie*

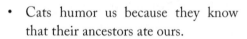

- Cats humor us because they know that their ancestors ate ours.

- The Cat's Philosophy: If you can't eat it, then shred it, sleep on it, or mate with it.

- A cat was courting his favorite feline. "I would die for you," he proclaimed. She replied, "How many times?"

- A black-and-white cat crossed my path this morning. Since then my luck has been patchy.

- A cat found a mysterious sweater, but the mystery was soon unraveled.

- A little boy was with his dad looking at a litter of kittens. Upon returning home, the little boy could not wait to tell his mother that there were two girl kittens and two boy kittens.

  "How do you know?" asked his mother.

  The boy replied, "Daddy picked them up and looked underneath. I think it's printed on the bottom."

- There was a mathematician who added up numbers and always concluded by saying "plus a cat." For example, he would say, "The total amount is one-thousand-five-hundred plus a cat." Apparently he had an add-a-puss complex.

- A woman walked into the pet store. "I haven't got much money," she told the clerk, "so I'd like to know if you've any kittens you'll let go cheap."

    "I'd let them go cheep, ma'am," said the clerk, "but they prefer to go meow."

- *Man:* "I just ran over your cat, and I'd like to replace it."
  Boy: "Well, get busy. There's a mouse in the basement."

- *Woman:* Have you ever seen a catfish?
  Girl: Yes, I have.
  Woman: How did it hold the rod?

To My Dear Friend the Dog:

I'm so sorry that you have been sent to the dog pound for the lamp you did not break, the fish you did not eat, and the carpet that you did not wet. Things here at the house are calmer now, and just to show you that I have no hard feelings, I'm sending you a picture, so you'll always remember me.

Best Regards,
The Cat

Chew Toys

Cowboy star Roy Rogers went bathing in a creek. Along came a cat and began nibbling on one of Roy's brand-new boots, which his wife, Dale Evans, had given him as a gift.

Dale entered the scene and shooed the kitty away. She turned to her husband and, to the tune of "Chatanooga Choo Choo," sang, "Pardon me, Roy, is that the cat that chewed your new shoe?"

What Goes Around . . .

Jonathan, noted for his tact, was awakened one morning at four o'clock by his ringing telephone. "Your cat's yowling, and it's keeping me awake," screamed an irate voice.

Jonathan thanked the caller and politely asked his name before hanging up. The next morning at four o'clock, Jonathan called back his neighbor. "Sir," he said, "I don't have a cat."

Be Concise

A cat went to a Western Union office, took out a blank form, and wrote, "Meow, meow, meow, meow, meow, meow, meow, meow, meow."

The clerk examined the paper and told the cat, "There are only nine words here. You could send another *meow* for the same cost."

"But," the cat replied, "that would be silly."

17 Kitten around with Cat Jokes

Hee Hee Hee Hee

My husband said it was either the cat or him. I miss him sometimes.

—*Author Unknown*

Lying Saucer

A New England antiques dealer noticed a mangy cat lapping up milk from a rare porcelain saucer in front of the general store. He went inside and offered ten dollars for the cat, but the owner said the cat wasn't for sale. The savvy dealer explained that he enjoyed rescuing wayward cats and raised his offer to fifty dollars.

"It's a deal," said the proprietor as he pocketed the money.

"For that sum," said the connoisseur, "I'm sure you won't mind throwing in the saucer."

"No way," replied the owner, "that's my lucky saucer. It's helped me sell twenty-seven cats already this week."

Cat and Mouse Heaven

A cat died and went to Heaven. Saint Peter said to the cat, "You have had a difficult life and we would like to do something nice to welcome you to Heaven. What would make you comfortable and happy now that you have arrived in Heaven?"

The cat replied, "Yes, life was tough. I either had wood floors or concrete sidewalks to lie on. If I could have a nice fluffy pillow on which to curl up, I will be very happy."

Saint Peter told the cat, "A thick, fluffy pillow will be given to you, and may you rest well on your . . . uhm . . . cat-er-pillar."

Next in line to enter the pearly gates were six mice. They had much the same conversation about a tough life. They were telling Saint Peter how they were always being chased and had to run and hide. They said they would like something to help. Saint Peter suggested tiny roller skates. This made the mice very happy indeed.

After a time, Saint Peter decided he would check on the cat to see if he was happy and well cared for. He found the cat absolutely delighted. The cat said, "The comfort provided by the pillow couldn't be better, and the meals on wheels were delicious!"

Smarty Cat

A man followed a woman and her cat out of a movie theater. He asked her, "I don't mean to bother you, but I couldn't help noticing that your cat was sitting on your lap and was really into the movie. He cried at the right spots; he moved nervously in his seat at the boring parts. And he laughed like crazy at the funny parts. Didn't you find that unusual?"

"Yes," she replied, "I found it very unusual because he hated the book."

The Versatile Cat

A local business was looking for office help. They put a sign in the window, stating: "HELP WANTED. Must be able to type, must be good with a computer, and must be bilingual. We are an Equal Opportunity Employer."

A short time afterward, a cat trotted up to the window, saw the sign, and went inside. He looked at the receptionist, then walked over to the sign, looked at it, and meowed.

Getting the idea, the receptionist got the office manager. The office manager looked at the cat and was surprised, to say the least. However, the cat seemed determined, so he led him into the office. Inside, the cat jumped up on the chair and stared at the manager.

The manager said, "I can't hire you. The sign says you have to be able to type."

The cat jumped down, went to the typewriter, and proceeded to type out a perfect letter. He took out the page and gave it to the manager, then jumped back on the chair. The manager was stunned, but then told the cat, "The sign says you have to be good with a computer."

The cat jumped down again and went to the computer. Then he proceeded to demonstrate his expertise with various programs, produced a sample spreadsheet and database, and presented them to the manager. By this time the manager was totally dumbfounded. He looked at the cat and said, "I realize that you are a very intelligent cat and have some unique abilities. However, I *still* can't give you the job."

The cat jumped down, went to a copy of the sign, and put his paw on the sentences that told about being an Equal Opportunity Employer. The manager said, "Yes, but the sign also says that you have to be bilingual."

The cat looked the manager straight in the eye and said, "Woof!"

Scan Scam

A man entered a doctor's office, sweating profusely, breathing heavily, and asking for help. The doctor rushed him into an examination room, looked him over, and said, "You are terribly overweight and out of shape, and you need to start on a regimen of strict diet and exercise immediately."

The man became agitated. "I'm in excellent shape, and I want a second opinion."

The doctor went into the back room and came out with a cat. He placed the cat on the man's chest. The cat started walking from head to toe poking and sniffing the patient's body, and finally looked at the doctor and meowed. The doctor said, "The cat thinks that you're grotesquely overweight, too."

The man was still unwilling to accept his condition, so the doctor returned to the back room and came back with a black Labrador. The dog sniffed the patient's body, walked from head to toe, and finally looked at the doctor and barked. The doctor said, "The Lab thinks you're flabby and overweight, too."

Finally resigned to the diagnosis, the man thanked the doctor and asked how much he owed. "Five-hundred fifty dollars," replied the doctor.

"Five-hundred fifty dollars just to tell me I'm out of shape!" exclaimed the man.

"Well," said the doctor, "I would only have charged you fifty dollars for my initial diagnosis. The additional five-hundred dollars was for the PET scans—the CAT scan and Lab tests."

Knock-knock Jokes

Knock, knock.
Who's there?
A Cadillac.
A Cadillac who?
A Cadillac mean if you pull its tail.

Knock, knock.
Who's there?
Cattle.
Cattle who?
Cattle always purr when you stroke it.

Knock, knock.
Who's there?
Catgut.
Catgut who?
Catgut your tongue?

Knock, knock.
Who's there?
Catsup.
Catsup who?
Cats up in a tree, and we can't get her down.

18 Cats and Computers

After scolding one's cat, one looks into its face
and is seized by the ugly suspicion that it has understood
every word and has filed it for reference.
—*Charlotte Gray*

16 Ways a Cat is Like a Computer

- User friendly, although the control key will not always function
- Available in three sizes: mainframe, desktop, and (the smallest) laptop
- Portable, if placed in suitable transportation case
- Mouse driven
- Self-cleaning
- Sensitive interfaces
- Dual video and audio input
- Visual and audio output; wide-ranging sound card
- Can function in direct sunlight but keep away from water
- Energy-saving standby mode

- Self-recharging
- Instant transition between standby and full-power mode
- Requires annual checkup
- Minimal power consumption as compared to energy output
- Top of the line: Never any need to upgrade
- If you properly care for your unit, it will give you years of loyal service. Many users get a second unit, to enjoy the ability to run complex simulation games.

10 Clues That Your Cat Has Hacked into Your E-mail Password

- Your keyboard has traces of kitty litter and a strange territorial scent.
- Your mouse has teeth marks in it—and an aroma of tuna.
- You find you've been subscribed to strange newsgroups like recreationalcatnip.com and alt.cats.world.domination.
- You receive e-mail messages from some guy named Tiger.
- Your Web browser has a new home page, www.feline.com.
- Your out-box contains hate-mail messages to Apple Computer, Inc. about their release of "CyberDog."
- You keep finding new software around your house like CatPayTax and WarCatII.
- On Facebook you're known as the IronMouser.
- Your screen saver is now a picture of Garfield and your mouse pad a picture of the Cat in the Hat.
- Your kitty is wearing carpal-tunnel braces.

19 Cat-a-Lists

Some people say that cats are
sneaky, evil, and cruel.
True, and they have many other
fine qualities as well.
—*Missy Dizick*

The Name is the Game

Bringing home a new kitten is as joyful and exciting as bringing home a
baby. In both instances, you'll want to give the adorable creature the right
name. According to recent polls, here's a kitten caboodle of the most popular names for male and female cats in the United States:

Males	Females
1. Max	1. Chloe
2. Tigger	2. Lucy
3. Tiger	3. Molly
4. Smokey	4. Bella
5. Oliver	5. Sophie
6. Buddy	6. Princess
7. Charlie	7. Cleo
8. Simba	8. Angel
9. Sammy	9. Lily
10. Oscar	10. Maggie
11. Jack	11. Zoe

12. Sam	12. Samantha
13. Toby	13. Sasha
14. Lucky	14. Gracie
15. Shadow	15. Misty
16. Simon	16. Callie
17. Milo	17. Daisy
18. Leo	18. Kitty
19. Bailey	19. Missy
20. Jake	20. Jasmine

Cat Bumper Snickers

- I Am Cat. Hear Me Roar!
- Children Are for People Who Can't Have Cats.
- I Got Rid of My Husband. The Cat Was Allergic.
- Cats Regard People as Warm-Blooded Furniture.
- I'm the Boss. My Cat Says So.
- It's My Cat's House. I Just Pay the Mortgage.
- It's My Cat's World. I'm Just Here to Run the Can Opener.
- Love Me; Love My Cat.
- It's Twelve Midnight: Do You Know What Your Cat Is Shredding?
- Every Dog Has His Day, But the Nights Are Reserved for Cats.
- We're Staying Together for the Sake of the Cats.

- My Cat Owns *Me*.
- Dogs Think They Are Humans. Cats Think They Are Gods.
- I Was a Cat in My Other Lives.
- The Four Cat Food Groups: Dry, Canned, Natural, Yours.
- If You Don't Like My Attitude, You Should See My Cat's.
- When Cats Have Hissy Fits, They Get into *Pfssst* Fights.
- Leading Libertarians Is Like Herding Cats.
- Think outside the Litter Box.
- It's Always Darkest Just Before You Step on the Cat.
- I'd Love to, But I Have to Floss My Cat.
- McDonald's Hamburger: $1.50. Can of Cat Food: $3.25. Hmmm.
- Hey, Dog! New Law: Red Light Means "Go."
- *Vet* Is a Four-Letter Word.
- Some Days You Are the Cat. Some Days You Are the Litter.
- I Neutered My Cat. Now He's a Consultant.
- You Can't Beat Purr-Fection.

Feline Favorites

- *favorite color:* purrple
- *favorite foods:* mice cream and Mice Krispies
- *favorite university:* Purrdue
- *favorite car:* a Catillac

- *favorite American presidents:* Thomas Jeffurson, William Henry and Benjamin Hairyson, Zachary Tailor, James Garfield, William Meoward Taft, Bite Eisenhowler, Richard Nips'em, and George H.W. and George W. Bushy Tail

- *favorite Chinese leader:* Meow Tse Tongue

- *favorite singers:* Cat Stevens and Eartha Kitten

- *favorite nursery rhyme:* "Three Blind Mice"

- *favorite Christmas songs:* "I Saw Mommy Hiss at Santa Claus," "Wreck the Halls"

- *favorite musical: Cats* (what else?)

- *favorite James Bond character:* Pussy Galore

- *favorite magazines: Good Mousekeeping*

- *favorite newspaper:* the *Washington Scratching Post*

- *favorite comic strips: Garfield* and *The Cats-enjammer Kids*

- *favorite books: The Great Cats-by* and *Cat-cher in the Rye*

- *favorite advice column:* "Dear Tabby"

- *favorite building:* the mew-see-em

- *favorite mountains:* the Catskills

- *favorite island:* Catalina

- *favorite part of the world:* the Purrsian Gulf

Chapter 19

My Cat's So Fat That . . .

- He has more chins than lives.
- She waits for a third bowl of food before she gets finicky.
- He no longer cleans himself unless coated with 9 Lives.
- I've been waiting fifteen months for her to have her dozen kittens.
- He only catches mice that get sucked into his gravitational pull.
- Her ginormous gut keeps the hardwood floors shiny. The cat isn't buffed, but the floors sure are.
- When he lies around the house, he lies *around* the house.
- She was in the Macy's Day parade, wearing ropes.
- He has his own ZIP code.
- When she walks along the beach, the tide comes in.
- Confused guests keep mistaking him for a beanbag chair.
- Whenever I try to lift her, my back goes out—and my back goes out more than she does.
- I've retrofitted the cat door with a garage door opener. Now Saint Bernards can enter.
- When he jumps into bed with me, I roll in his direction.
- I've noted an upsurge in collapsed furniture and broken branches.
- The sand in the litter box is starting to turn to glass.

Politically Correct Terms for Cat Owners

My cat didn't "get fixed." I prefer to call a spayed a spayed. Here's some politically correct straight talk about my cat:

- My cat does not fear dogs. She simply uses them as sprint practice facilitators.

- My cat is not a "treat-seeking missile." He enjoys the proximity of food.

- My cat does not gobble. She takes in nutrients at a high rate of efficiency.

- My cat does not barf hair balls. He is a rug redecorator.

- My cat does not scratch. She is a furniture skin ventilator.

- My cat does not yowl. He sings the song of Nature.

- My cat is not a "shedding machine." She is a hair relocation stylist.

- My cat is not a bed hog. He is a mattress appreciator.

- My cat is not a chatterbox. She is advising me on what to do next.

- My cat is not a substance abuser. He is catnip appreciative.

- My cat is not a "lap fungus." She is bed selective.

- My cat is not a pest. He is an attention seeker.

- My cat is not a ruthless hunter. She is a vermin control expert.

- My cat is not hydrophobic. He has an inability to appreciate moisture.

- My cat is not underfoot. She is shepherding me to my next destination (which is probably the food dish).

20 Have You Heard?

Of all domestic animals
the cat is the most expressive.
His face is capable of showing
a wide range of expressions.
His tail is a mirror of his mind.
His gracefulness is
surpassed only by his agility.
And, along with all these,
he has a sense of humor.

—*Walter Chandoha*

Have you heard about the tailor who let his cat out, the firefighter who put her cat out, and the private eye who put a tail on a Manx?

Have you heard about the cat who entertained herself with some wool? *After a while, she had a ball.* Have you heard what happened when she swallowed that ball? *She had mittens. All her offspring were born wearing sweaters.*

I hope you found this yarn to be a fine example of knit-wit. Here are some other cats that you might have heard about:

Have you heard about . . .

- the angry cat? *She threw a hissy fit.*

- the grumpy cat? *He was a sour puss.*

- the curious cat? *He was a peeping tom.*

- the silent cat? *She was the victim of a purr snatcher.*

- the psychic cat? *He was adopted from the E.S.P.C.A.*

- the sensitive cat? *She cried over spilt milk.*
- the dyslexic cat? *He cried, "Woem, weom!"*
- the cat who had eight kittens? *She was an octopus.*
- the cowardly felines? *Their names were Scaredy and Fraidy.*
- the cat who swallowed a duck? *He was a down-in-the-mouth, duck-filled fatty puss.*
- the cat who had a hairball? *She couldn't hack it.*
- the cat who was a comedian? *His name was Groucho Manx.*
- the old cat who became forgetful and stopped making any sounds? *She developed a purr-senility disorder.*
- the golf-playing cat? *Even without a catty he consistently scored fur under purr.*
- the adolescent cat? *She pleaded with her parents, "Why don't you let me lead one of my own lives?"*
- the cat who liked to lounge around the stereo? *He hoped to catch the tweeter for lunch, unless the woofer got him first.*
- the cat who got hurt? *She whimpered, "Me ow!"*
- the cat who was walking the beach on Christmas Eve? *He had Sandy Claws.*
- the cat who ate some cheese and then sat by a mousehole? *She waited with baited breath.*
- the radioactive cat? *He had eighteen half-lives.*
- the cat who chased a mouse through the screen door? *They both strained themselves.*

- the cat who robbed McDonald's and Wendy's? *She was a cat burgerlar.*
- the cat named Ben-Hur? *It used to be called Ben, until it had kittens.*
- the cat who caught a bird? *He enjoyed a breakfast of shredded tweet.*
- the fast cat? *She put quicksand in her litter box.*
- the cat who tried to find out why his humans forgot to place cat litter in his box? *He didn't have anything to go on.*
- the teeny-tiny cat? *She drank only condensed milk.*
- the cat who loved to bowl? *He was an alley cat.*
- the alley cat who married a chicken? *They had a peeping tom.*
- the cat who married a tree? *They had a catalog.*
- the cat who climbed the drapes? *She had good claws to do it—and she started from scratch.*
- the cat with chutzpah? *He was a pushy cat.*
- the cat who swallowed a bag of coins? *There was money in that kitty.*
- the obese, ill-tempered, talkative cat? *He was a flabby, crabby, gabby tabby.*
- the mother cat looking for her straying kittens? *Like a poet, she listened for their mews.*
- the feline who impeded the iceman's work? *The cat got his tong.*
- the baby cat who joined the Red Cross? *She wanted to be a first-aid kit.*
- the two cats who raced each other to the milk bowl? *One beat the other by a lap.*

- the kindle of cats named Johann Christian, Wilhelm Friedemann, Johann Sebastian, and Carl Philipp Emanuel? *They were all born in a litter Bachs.*

- the man who was afraid of cats? *He had catatonia, clawstrophobia, and purranoia.*

- the woman who refused to spay and neuter her cats? *She was arrested for kitty littering.*

- the man who saw a sign at a pet store that said "Free Cats"? *So he went in and did.*

- the unemployed cat burglar from Nepal? *What else can a Katmandu?*

21 Hey Diddle Diddle, the Cat in the Riddle

A cat's a cat and that's that.
—*American Folk Saying*

When does the weather go "Splash, splash, meow! woof!"?
When it's raining cats and dogs.

What's even worse than raining cats and dogs?
Hailing taxicabs.

What do you say when it starts to drizzle?
"Its raining kittens and puppies."

What do cats and dogs say during the holidays?
"Have a meowy Christmas and a yappy New Year!"

What's the difference between a cat and a comma?
A cat has paws at the end of its claws, and a comma is a pause at the end of a clause.

What's the difference between a frog and a cat?
A frog croaks all the time, a cat just nine times.

What happened to the guy whose cat got run over by a steamroller?
He just stood there with a long puss.

How do you keep your cat from sleeping in bed with you?
You do what you have to if puss comes to shove.

What do cats call their mother's father?
  Grandpaw.

Why did the cat give birth on the side of the road?
  Because the sign said "Fine for Littering."

What kind of formal dances do cats have?
  Hair balls.

Why is a cat drinking milk like a track star?
  Because they both enjoy taking a few laps.

Why are cats poor dancers?
  Because they have two left feet.

Where is one place that your cat can sit, but you can't?
  Your lap.

What happened when the Frenchman tried to teach his three young kittens how to swim by throwing them in a lake?
  Un, deux, trois cats sank.

What did the cat say when his tail got caught in a lawn mower?
  "It won't be long now."

What did the cat say as she rescued her daughter from the violin factory?
  "I didn't raise my daughter to be fiddled with."

When do cats and dogs get along together?
  When you have hot dogs with catsup.

What kind of work does a weak cat do?
Light mousework.

Why don't cats play poker in the jungle?
Too many cheetahs.

Why are cats better than babies?
Because you have to change a litter box only once a day.

Where does a cat go when it loses its tail?
The retail store.

Why did the judge dismiss the entire jury made up of cats?
Because each of them was guilty of purr-jury.

What do you call the DNA genome for felines?
Helix the cat.

What do you get when you cross a cat with a parrot?
A carrot.

What do you get if you cross a cat and a gorilla?
An animal that puts YOU out a night!

How many cats does it take to change a lightbulb?
Cats do not change lightbulbs. People change lightbulbs. So, the real question is: "How long will it be before I can expect some light, some dinner, and a massage?"

Truths and Falsehoods about Cats 22

> Intelligence in the
> cat is underrated.
> —*Louis Wain*

What did one cat say to the other while watching a tennis match? "My mother's in that racket." Har, har—but before cat lovers experience a high-strung gut reaction, they should know that *catgut* is a misnomer. Cats aren't killed to manufacture the tough cords for violins and tennis strings; catgut is actually made from the intestines of sheep, and sometimes horses, cattle, and mules.

Test your knowledge of other old wives' tales of cats that may be true or false:

• *Cats are solitary creatures and prefer to live alone.* False. Although no cat would admit it, cats lead healthier, more contented lives if there is another friendly cat in the house. Close cat buddies groom each other to create healthier coats and ears. Cat families usually play best in even numbers.

• *Cats are color-blind.* False. Recent studies show that, contrary to popular belief, cats can see blue, green, and red.

• *Cats spend most of their lives sleeping.* True. Kittens are born with their eyes shut. They open them in about six days, take a look around, then close them again for the better part of their natural lives. A cat spends nearly 30 percent of its life grooming itself and about two-thirds of its life catnapping and catsleeping. On average, humans sleep seven and a half hours a day while cats snooze sixteen hours each day. No other animal spends more time asleep except opossums and bats.

- *A purring cat is a happy cat.* Sometimes false. Purring is sometimes heard in cats who are severely ill or anxious, perhaps as a self-soothing vocalization. But, more typically, purring is a sign of contentment, first heard in kittens as they suckle milk from their mother.

- *Cats always land on their feet.* Usually true. Cats have exceptional co-ordination and balance, a tail that acts like a gyroscope, and a flexible musculoskeletal system. They are normally able to orient their bodies in space in such a way as to land on all four limbs. But if they fall from a great height, their "righting instinct" may not be enough to save them from bodily harm.

- *All cats are born with blue eyes.* True. A large majority of white cats with blue eyes are deaf. White cats with one blue eye are deaf only in the ear closer to that blue eye.

- *Many people are allergic to cat fur.* False. People who are allergic to cats are actually allergic to a protein in cat saliva. If the cat is bathed regularly, allergic people have better tolerance to it.

- *People universally believe that black cats are bad luck.* False. Black cat superstitions originated in America. In Asia and England, a black cat is considered lucky. "A fisherman's wife who keeps black cats will ensure her husband's return," promises an English proverb.

- *Cats can't sweat.* True. A cat will never break a sweat because it has no sweat glands. Rather, when they are overheated, cats lick their fur vigorously, spreading saliva over their bodies to act as a cooling agent.

- *There's little difference between dog food and cat food.* False. Cats must have fat in their diet, because they can't produce it on their own. Never feed your cat dog food, because cats need different amounts of protein, fats, and certain types of amino acids than dogs do.

- *Provide water for your dog and milk for your cat.* False. Believe it or not, many cats are lactose intolerant, unable to properly digest cow's milk. Milk and milk products give them diarrhea.

- *Cats hate to be immersed in water.* Generally true. The ancestors of modern cats were desert animals, where water was scarce, so they didn't grow accustomed to it. But some wild cats, especially tigers, love to swim, and kittens who grow up exposed to water generally don't mind it.

23 Famous Cats and Cat Lovers

No matter how cats fight,
there are always
plenty of kittens.
—*Abraham Lincoln*

White House Cats

The title of this section refers not to housecats that are white, but to cats in the White House, where a number of cats have deigned to share residence with presidents:

- Secretary of State William H. Seward presented Abraham Lincoln with two kittens early in his administration. Treasury official Maunsell B. Field wrote: "Mr. Lincoln possessed extraordinary kindness of heart when his feelings could be reached. He was fond of dumb animals, especially cats." During a conference with General Ulysses Grant and Admiral David Porter, the president was interrupted by the meowing of three motherless kittens. Picking them up and placing them on his lap, the president said: "Poor little creatures, don't cry; you'll be taken care of." Grant aide Horace Porter recalled that it was a "curious sight at an army headquarters, upon the eve of a great military crisis" to watch the commander-in-chief "tenderly caressing three stray kittens. It well illustrated the kindness of the man's disposition, and showed the child-like simplicity which was mingled with the grandeur of his nature."

- Theodore Roosevelt favored Slippers, so named because the gray cat had an extra toe on each paw. The president allowed the cat to appear at diplomatic dinners. One day a sleeping Slippers was blocking the hallway to one of those state dinners, and everyone had to walk around the snoozing tabby.

- Calvin Coolidge's cats—Tiger, Blacky, Bounder, and Climber—would lounge around his neck and cleave to his clothing as the president walked around the White House.

- Morris, the Purina 9Lives cat, was discovered at an animal shelter in New England. In 1973, Morris's cat-food commercials won him the coveted Patsy, the "animal Oscar." The orange tabby charmer eventually became honorary director of StarKist Foods, with veto power over any cat-food flavor he didn't like. President Richard M. Nixon invited Morris to cosign (with a paw print) the National Animal Protection Bill.

Cats Throughout History

In front of every great cat stands a man or woman who takes all the credit. Here's a gallery of historical figures who had the good sense to love their cats:

- The prophet Muhammad adored cats. According to Islamic legend, Muhammad was called to a meeting but did not want to wake up his cat Muezza, who had fallen asleep in his arms. So the prophet cut off his sleeve and left behind the peacefully snoozing Muezza.

- Cardinal Richelieu was so fond of cats that he shared his Versailles home with fourteen of them. Specially appointed attendants cared for them and built a "cattery" for the cats to live in. Upon his death, the cardinal left all his worldly wealth to his feline companions.

- Sir Isaac Newton, who first described the principle of gravity, also invented the swinging cat door. To avoid interruptions to his work and to enhance the convenience and independence of his many cats, the great scientist and philosopher fashioned the first cat flap.

- Florence Nightingale owned more than sixty cats in her lifetime and often complained about mysterious "stains" on her paperwork.

- Winston Churchill adored cats. He used to refer to his cat Jock as his "special assistant." The tabby attended cabinet meetings, and dinner could not begin until the pampered pet joined Churchill at the table. Jock was reported to be on the bed with his master on the day the great British statesman died.

- All of the personages above have experienced ailurophilia, the love of cats. Ailurophobia is the fear of cats. Genghis Khan, Alexander the Great, Julius Caesar, Henry II, Charles XI, Napoleon, and Adolf Hitler all suffered from this condition and would nearly faint in the presence of a cat.

Authors like cats because they are such
quiet, lovable, wise creatures,
and cats like authors for the same reasons.
—*Robertson Davies*

Ailurophilia appears to be a congenital condition of writers. Humorist Dan Greenberg quips, "Cats are dangerous companions for writers because cat watching is a near-perfect method of writing avoidance." Nonetheless, writers have had a great deal to say about their feline companions:

- You are my cat, and I am your human.—*Hilaíre Belloc*

- A kitten is a rosebud in the garden of the animal kingdom.—*Robert Southey*

- Our perfect companions never have fewer than four feet.—*Colette*

- Time spent with cats is never wasted—*Colette*

- There are no ordinary cats.—*Colette*

- Cats are a mysterious kind of folk. There is more passing in their minds than we are aware of.—*Sir Walter Scott*

- Like those great sphinxes lounging through eternity in noble attitude upon the desert sand, they gaze incuriously at nothing, calm and wise. Drowsing, they dream dreams that have no end.—*Charles Baudelaire*

- It is a very inconvenient habit of kittens . . . that, whatever you say to them, they *always* purr.—*Lewis Carroll*

- He lies there, purring and dreaming, shifting his limbs now and then, in an ecstasy of cushioned comfort. He seems the incarnation of everything soft and silky and velvety.—*Saki (Hector Hugh Munro)*

- A cat has emotional honesty. Human beings, for one reason or another, may hide their feelings, but the cat does not.—*Ernest Hemingway*

- A cat can be trusted to purr when she is pleased, which is more than can be said for human beings.—*William Inge*

- A cat isn't fussy—just so long as you remember he likes his milk in a shallow, rose-patterned saucer, and his fish in the blue plate. From which he will take it and eat it off the floor.—*Arthur Bridges*

- If a fish is the movement of water embodied, given shape, then a cat is a diagram and pattern of subtle air.—*Doris Lessing*

- Cats are only human; they have their faults.—*Kingsley Amis*

Many a famous writer has become a cat collector:

- "What greater gift than the love of a cat?" exclaimed Charles Dickens (author of *A Tail of Two Kitties*). A nearly deaf white cat was Dickens's constant companion. Dickens named his friend simply The Master's Cat, because the animal followed him everywhere.

- Edgar Allan Poe took his cat Catarina everywhere. She sat on his shoulder as he wrote and inspired his short story "The Black Cat." In 1840, Poe published an essay extolling the value of animal instinct over human intelligence.

- Mark Twain kept eleven cats, including Blatherskite, Sour Mash, and Stray Kit, at his farm in Connecticut. According to his daughter Susy, "The difference between Papa and Mamma is that Mamma loves morals and Papa loves cats." According to Twain, "Of all God's creatures there is only one that cannot be made the slave of the leash. That one is the cat. If man could be crossed with the cat, it would improve man, but deteriorate the cat."

- Harriet Beecher Stowe took in a stray Maltese named Calvin, who sat on her shoulder as she wrote her books, including *Uncle Tom's Cabin*.

- Edward Lear, the English popularizer of the limerick form of poetry, adored his tabby Foss, rumored to be the inspiration of Lear's famous children's poem "The Owl and the Pussycat." The pair lived together in an Italian villa for almost fifteen years before Foss passed on. Lear followed two months after.

- In Lewis Carroll's fantasy *Alice's Adventures in Wonderland*, the Cheshire Cat tells the heroine: "Well, then, you see a dog growls when it's angry, and wags its tail when it's pleased. Now *I* growl when I'm pleased, and wag my tail when I'm angry. Therefore I'm mad." "*I* call it purring, not growling," said Alice. "Call it what you like," said the Cat.

- Ernest Hemingway shared his Key West home with more than thirty cats. "One cat just leads to another," he wrote. The Hemingways so trusted their yellow-eyed cat Mr. Feather Puss that they allowed him to babysit their infant.

- "When a cat adopts you, there is nothing to be done about it except to put up with it and wait until the wind changes," advised the poet and critic T. S. Eliot. In 1939, Eliot published *Old Possum's Book of Practical Cats*. The book inspired the Broadway musical *Cats*, featuring the music of Andrew Lloyd Webber. After the poet's death in 1965, the composer approached Eliot's widow, Valerie, for permission to use the poems in the musical. Valerie Eliot granted permission with one condition: Webber couldn't rewrite a word of the original poems. In 1982, *Cats* leaped from London to New York and has become one of the longest-running shows ever. In 1948, Eliot won the Nobel Prize for Literature, but he is today more remembered for *Cats* than for the rest of his prodigious literary output.

A special kind of populist literature is the comic strip, and the cats we meet in our funny pages and on our movie screens exert great force on our collective imagination:

- In 1910, George Herriman created the cartoon character Krazy Kat and her sidekick, the brick-throwing Ignatz Mouse. This first of all cartoon cats starred in an animated feature in 1916.

- In 1917, Pat Sullivan and Otto Messmer introduced Thomas Kat, the prototype of Felix the Cat. Felix starred in the first "talkie" cartoon, a year before Mickey Mouse began to squeak his dialog. Felix was also the subject of the very first television test broadcasts in 1928 and was

NBC's official test pattern into the late 1930s. He was the first cartoon character to be made into a balloon for a parade.

- Starting in 1940, the ever-dueling duo Tom and Jerry have chased each other from the Hollywood Bowl to Hungary to outer space and back, and they're still going strong. Tom, the cat, and Jerry, the mouse, have won seven Best Short Subject Academy Awards. *Tom and Jerry* seem to be the model for the more ghoulish *Itchy* (the mouse) & *Scratchy* (the cat) animated cartoon that is part of the long-running animated series *The Simpsons*.

- In 1945, Sylvester J. Pussycat, better known as simply Sylvester the Cat, first starred in the Warner Bros. "Life With Feathers" television cartoon episode. The lisping Sylvester ("Thufferin' thuccotash!") appeared in more than ninety animated cartoons and won three Academy Awards. The name "Sylvester" is a play on *silvestris*, the scientific name for the domestic cat species. Sylvester's voice is a version of Daffy Duck's.

- The Cat in the Hat, a creation of Theodor Seuss Geisel, who called himself "Dr. Seuss," first appeared in the children's book of the same name published in 1957. With his simple and often single-syllable vocabulary, the good Doctor knew how to encourage children to read and have fun in the process.

- "Way down deep, we're all motivated by the same urges. Cats have the courage to live by them," said Jim Davis. That's why, in 1978, Davis created the enduringly popular comic strip cat Garfield. Within four years *Garfield* was appearing in a thousand newspapers around the world.

25 A Cat's Garden of Verses

Like a graceful vase, a cat,
even when motionless, seems to flow.
—*George Will*

Gather kittens
while you may.
Time brings
only sorrow;
And the kittens
of today
Will be old cats
tomorrow.
—*Oliver Herford*

Ode to Cats

You see the beauty of the world
Through eyes of unalloyed content,
And in my study chair upcurled,
Move me to pensive wonderment.

I wish I knew your trick of thought,
The perfect balance of your ways.
They seem an inspiration, caught
From other laws in older days.

An Alphabet of Cats

Acrobats in furry coats.
Believe they own you.
Connoisseurs of comfort.
Dogs drool, cats rule.
Eager to be adopted.
Furballs and foibles.
Great mousekeepers.
Hate to be disturbed.
I purr, therefore I am.
Juggle busy schedules.
Knead you.
Love to bring "gifts."
Make no apologies.
Never have bad hair days.
One is rarely enough.
Paws-itively purr-fect.
Quick on the claw.
Rodent wranglers.
Sandpaper kisses.
"**T**he dog did it."
Use reverse psychology.
Vivacious after catnip.
Wash away the blues.
Xalt in clean litter boxes.
Yoga and nap masters.
Zig zag through nine lives!

—Meiji Stewart

Chapter 25

A Cat's Wish

A plate of fish, a cozy lap,
Perhaps a lick of cream—
To sit and purr before the fire,
Well, even cats can dream!

I've never had a proper home,
No door has opened wide,
Or friendly voice called out to me,
"Come, puss, come on inside."

But now I may have found a friend;
Though I'm not really sure.
I dare not eat the food she brings,
Until she's closed the door.

But there's a nice big wooden box,
Put just inside the shed,
With cozy blanket tucked well in,
To make a lovely bed.

Tomorrow I shall take a chance
(She seems so nice and kind.)
To get myself inside that door
And leave the dark behind.

That friendly fire I'll sit beside,
My lonely days all past.
A real belonging cat I'll be,
And have a home at last.

But there are other lonely ones
Who ask themselves "Why me?"
If only they would have my luck
So happy I would be.

Last Words to a Dumb Friend

Pet was never mourned as you,
Purrer of the spotless hue—
Plumy tail and wistful gaze,
While you humored our queer ways.

Never another pet for me.
Let your place all vacant be.
                    —*Thomas Hardy*

Epitaph in a Pet Cemetery

No, heaven will not ever heaven be,
Unless my cats are there to welcome me.

26 Nursery Rhyme Cats

**It's better to feed one cat
than many mice.**
—*Norwegian Proverb*

Read the following nursery rhyme and then
answer the question posed in the last line:

As I was going to St. Ives,
I met a man with seven wives.
Every wife had seven sacks.
Every sack had seven cats.
Every cat had seven kits.
Kits, cats, sacks, wives—
How many were going to St. Ives?

The answer to the question is . . . one. While the man and his wives and
their sacks, cats, and kits were going *from* St. Ives, only the speaker—the *I*
in the rhyme—was going *to* St. Ives.

As in the ditty above, cats and kits are so much a part of our lives that
they live in our children's nursery rhymes. Can you supply the missing line
in each of the following classic verses from our childhood?

1. Hey, diddle, diddle,

   _____,
   The cow jumped over the moon.
   The little dog laughed
   To see such sport,
   And the dish ran away with the spoon.

2. _____?
   I've been to London to visit the Queen.
   Pussycat, pussycat, what did you there?
   I frightened a little mouse under her chair.

3. _____,
   They lost their mittens,
   And they began to cry,
   Oh, mother, dear,
   We sadly fear,
   Our mittens we have lost.

4. Ding dong bell!
   _____!

   Who put her in?
   Little Tommy Lin.

5. Little Robin Redbreast sat upon a tree,

   _____.

   Down came pussycat, and away Robin ran,
   Said Little Robin Redbreast, "Catch me if you can."

6. There was a crooked man, and he walked a crooked mile.
   He found a crooked sixpence against a crooked stile.

   _____.

   And they all lived together in a little crooked house.

7. _____

In a beautiful pea-green boat
They took some honey, and plenty of money,
Wrapped up in a five-pound note.
                                    —*Edward Lear*

Answers

1. The cat and the fiddle 2. Pussycat, pussycat, where have you been 3. Three little kittens 4. Pussy's in the well 5. Up went pussycat and down went he 6. He had a crooked cat which caught a crooked mouse 7. The Owl and the Pussycat went to sea

Cats Going out on a Limerick **27**

Since each of us is blessed with only one life,
why not live it with a cat?
—*Robert Stearns*

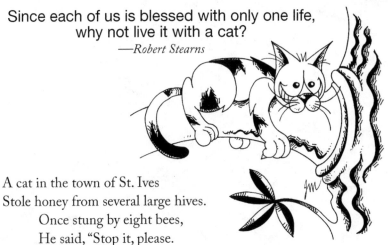

A cat in the town of St. Ives
Stole honey from several large hives.
　　Once stung by eight bees,
　　He said, "Stop it, please.
You know I have only nine lives!"

There once were two cats of Kilkenny;
Each thought there was one cat too many.
　　So they scratched and they fit,
　　And they tore and they bit,
Till instead of two, there weren't any.

Said a cat as he playfully threw
His wife down a well in Peru,
　　"Relax, dearest Dora,
　　Please don't be Angora.
I was only Artesian you."

There was an old bulldog named Caesar,
Who went for a cat just to tease her;
    But she spat and she spit,
    Till the old bulldog quit.
Now when poor Caesar sees her, he flees her.

There was a kind curate of Kew
Who kept a large cat in a pew.
    There he taught it each week
    A new letter of Greek,
But it never got further than mu.

A Cat's Night Before Christmas 28

(with thanks to Clement Clarke Moore)

'Twas the night before Christmas, and all
    through the house
Not a creature was stirring, not even a
    mouse.
We kitties were snuggled, all tucked in our
    beds,
While visions of cat goodies danced in our
    heads.

Our stockings were hung by the cat bowls with care,
In hopes that old Santa Claws soon would be there.
And mamma in her cat collar and I in my cap,
Had just settled down for a long winter's nap.

When out on the lawn there arose such a clatter,
I sprang from my bed to see what was the matter.
Away to the window I flew like a flash.
I opened the shutters and slashed up the sash.

The moon on the breast of the new-fallen snow
Gave the luster of midday to objects below.
When out on the rooftop, the noise was so purry
I knew furry Santa Claws was in a hurry.

And what to my lovely blue eyes should appear
But Santa himself in his full cat sled gear.
More rapid than cheetahs his coursers they came,
And he whistled and shouted and called them by name.

"Now Tabatha! Felix! Now Tommy and Muffy!
On Mittens! On Spitfire! On Rascal and Fluffy!
To the top of the porch! To the top of the wall!
Now dash away! Dash away! Dash away all!"

As dry leaves that before the wild hurricane fly,
When they meet with an obstacle, mount to the sky,
So up to the housetop the coursers they flew,
With the sleigh full of cat toys, and Santa Claws, too.

And then, in a twinkling, I heard, to my awe,
The prancing and scratching of each little claw.
Old Santa Claws purred, through the kitty door went.
Then he stopped and he sniffed, and he picked up a scent.

The cat treats we left him were by the back door.
We kitties had baked them an hour before.
He set about working, with nary a sigh,
And filled up the stockings with cat toys piled high.

And white-bearded Santa Claws, jolly and fat,
Hauled a bag full of presents, and all for a cat.
"The best Christmas ever!" I thought with a purr,
Then I coughed up a hair ball and shed some more fur.

Claws waved once at me with his mighty cat paw.
Although I was hiding, my black nose he saw.
He flew out the kitty door, in such a rush,
Jumped right on his cat sled and howled out, "Mush! Mush!"

The eight Maine coon cat team was raring to go.
Their paws had grown chilly, as they stood on the snow.
I heard Santa exclaim, as he rose out of sight:
"Meowy Christmas to all, and to cats a good life!"

29 Cat Haiku

I love cats. I love their grace and their elegance.
I love their independence and their arrogance,
and the way they lie and look at you, summing you up,
surely to your detriment, with that unnerving,
unwinking, appraising stare.

—*Joyce Stranger*

You never feed me.
Perhaps I'll sleep on your face.
That will sure show you.

The rule for today:
Touch my tail, I shred your hand.
New rule tomorrow.

Grace personified,
I leap into the window.
I meant to do that.

Blur of motion, then—
Silence, me, a paper bag.
What is so funny?

You're always typing.
Well, let's see you ignore my
Sitting on your hands.

My small cardboard box.
You cannot see me if I
Can just hide my head.

Terrible battle.
I fought for hours. Come and see!
What's a "term paper"?

I wanna go out.
Oh, drat! Help! I got outside!
I wanna go in!

Small brave carnivores
Kill pinecones and mosquitoes.
Fear vacuum cleaner.

Chapter 29

Oh, no! The Big One
Has been trapped by newspaper!
Cat to the rescue!

Cats howl in lament:
"Thumbs! If only we had thumbs!
We could break so much!"

The Big Ones snore now.
Every room is dark and cold
Time for Cup Hockey.

Step on No Pets 30

Most cats,
when they are out,
want to be in,
and vice versa,
and often simultaneously.
—*Louis J. Camuti*

A palindrome is a word, like *level*; a compound, like *senile felines*; or a sentence, like the title of this chapter, that communicates the same message when the letters of which it is composed are read in reverse order. Cast your eyes upon the dozen most elegant sentence palindromes that include cats:

STACK CATS.

TACKLE ELK CAT.

WOE ME: "MEOW!"

WAS IT A CAT I SAW?

PURR. IT'S A STIRRUP.

SO, CATNIP IN TACOS?

NO, SIT! CAT ACT IS ON.

WE MOOCH, COO, MEW.

REP PUSSY ASSAYS SUPPER.

SENILE FEMALES. RODNEY AWAY, ENDORSE LAME FELINES.

PUSS, A LEGACY RAT IN A SNUG, UNSANITARY CAGE, LASS UP.

ARE WE NOT DRAWN ONWARD, TACO CAT, DRAWN ONWARD TO NEW ERA?

111

31 Hamlet's Cat's Soliloquy

Tabbý—or not Tabbý
To go outside, and there perchance to stay,
Or to remain within—that is the question:

Whether 'tis nobler for a cat to suffer
The cuffs and buffets of inclement weather
That Nature rains on those who roam abroad,
Or take a nap upon a scrap of carpet,
And so by dozing melt the solid hours
That clog the clock's bright gears with sullen time
And stall the dinner bell.

To sit, to stare outdoors, and by a stare
To seem to state a wish to venture forth
Without delay. Then when the portal's opened,
To stand transfixed by paralyzing doubt.
To prowl; to sleep; to choose not knowing when
We may once more our readmittance gain—
Aye, there's the hair ball;

For if a paw were shaped to turn a knob,
Or work a lock or slip a window catch,
And going out and coming in were made
As simple as the breaking of a bowl.
What cat would bear the household's petty plagues—
The cook's well-practiced kicks, the butler's broom,

The infant's careless pokes, the trampled tail,
And all the daily shocks that fur is heir to?
Would that he, would of his own free will,
His mighty exodus or entrance make
With a mere mitten.

Who would spaniels fear,
Or strays trespassing from a neighbor's yard,
But that the dread of our unheeded cries
And scratches at a barricaded door
No claw can open up dispel our nerve
And make us rather bear our humans' faults
Than run away to unguessed miseries?

Thus caution doth make house cats of us all;
And thus the bristling hair of resolution
Is softened up with the pale brush of thought,
And since our choices hinge on weighty things,
We pause upon the threshold of decision.

—Well, I am Shakespaw

32 The Quotable Cat

Humorists on Cats

The principal difference between a cat and a lie is that a cat only has nine lives.

—*Mark Twain*

That cat will write her autograph all over your leg if you let her.

—*Mark Twain*

I gave my cat a bath the other day. He enjoyed it, and it was fun for me. The fur would stick to my tongue, but other than that . . .

—*Steve Martin*

To bathe a cat takes brute force, perseverance, courage of conviction, and a cat. The last ingredient is usually hardest to come by.

—*Stephen Baker*

I've always wanted to give birth. To kittens. I figure it would hurt less, and when you're done, you'd have kittens!

—Betsy Salkind

It's easy to understand why the cat has eclipsed the dog as modern America's favorite pet. People like pets to possess the same qualities they do. Cats are irresponsible and recognize no authority, yet are completely dependent on others for their material needs. Cats cannot be made to do anything useful. Cats are mean for the fun of it.

—P. J. O'Rourke

The best things in life are free. So, how many kittens do you want?

—Nancy Jo Perdue

Meow is like *aloha*—it can mean anything.

—Hank Ketchum

If toast always lands butter-side down and cats always land on their feet, what happens if you strap toast to the back of a cat and drop it?

—Steven Wright

My cat was up all night throwing up. So obviously I was up all night holding her hair.

—Sarah Silverman

I bought a generic cat. It only had five lives.

—Buzz Nutley

I don't get no respect. When I played in the sandbox, the cat kept covering me up.

—*Rodney Dangerfield*

I don't see the purpose of cats. Dogs can protect you, can sniff out things, and can be your eyes if you're blind. Could you imagine a seeing-eye cat? The first person who walks by with an untied shoelace, and you're history.

—*Christine O'Rourke*

Cats are intended to teach us that not everything in nature has a function.

—*Garrison Keillor*

If a cat does something, we call it instinct; if we do the same thing, for the same reason, we call it intelligence.

—*Will Cuppy*

But Seriously . . .

You become responsible, forever, for what you have tamed.

—*Antoine de Saint Exupéry*

I think it would be great to be a cat! You come and go as you please. People always feed and pet you. They don't expect much of you. You can play with them, and when you've had enough, you go away. You can pick and choose who you want to be around. You can't ask for more than that.

—*Patricia McPherson*

In his castle He is King and I his vassal.

—*Mildred R. Howland*

It is a matter to gain the affection of a cat. He is a philosophical animal, tenacious of his own habits, fond of order and neatness, and disinclined to extravagant sentiment. He will be your friend, if he finds you worthy of friendship, but not your slave.

—*Théophile Gautier*

The cat has too much spirit to have no heart.

—*Ernest Menaul*

The cat is a puzzle for which there is no solution.

—*Hazel Nicholson*

To escort a cat on a leash is against the nature of the cat.

—*Adlai Stevenson*

Work—other people's work—is an intolerable idea to a cat. Can you picture cats herding sheep or agreeing to pull a cart? They will not inconvenience themselves to the slightest degree.

—*Louis J. Camuti*

Two cats can live as cheaply as one, and their owner has twice as much fun.

—*Lloyd Alexander*

There are people who reshape the world by force or argument, but the cat just lies there, dozing; and the world quietly reshapes itself to suit his comfort and convenience.

—*Allen* and *Ivy Dodd*

There are two means of refuge from the miseries of life: music and cats.

—*Albert Schweitzer*

The phrase "domestic cat" is an oxymoron.

—*George Will*

Life + a cat adds up to an incalculable sum.

—*Rainer Maria Rilke*

A cat pours his body on the floor like water. It is restful just to see him.

—*William Lyon Phelps*

You will always be lucky if you know how to make friends with strange cats.

—*Colonial American proverb*

A cat is there when you call her—if she doesn't have something better to do.

—*Bill Adler*

The really great thing about cats is their endless variety. One can pick a cat to fit almost any kind of decor, color scheme, income, personality, mood. But under the fur; whatever color it may be, there still lies, essentially unchanged, one of the world's free souls.

—*Eric Gurney*

What is the appeal about cats? . . . They don't care if you like them. They haven't the slightest notion of gratitude, and they never pretend. They take what you have to offer, and away they go.

—*Mavis Gallant*

Cats know not how to pardon.

—*Jean de la Fontaine*

In the middle of a world that has always been a bit mad, the cat walks with confidence.

—*Roseanne Anderson*

Cats seem to go on the principle that it never does any harm to ask for what you want.

—*Joseph Wood Krutch*

Cats are rather delicate creatures and they are subject to a great many different ailments, but I never heard of one who suffered from insomnia.

—*Joseph Wood Krutch*

Even a cat is a lion in her own lair.

—Indian proverb

The cat is a lion in a jungle of small bushes.

—Indian proverb

A cat is always on the wrong side of the door.

—Author Unknown

There is no snooze button on a cat who wants breakfast.

—Author Unknown

A cat will be your friend, but never your slave.

—Théophile Gautier

The cat is a dilettante in fur.

—Théophile Gautier

I love cats because I love my home and little by little they become its visible soul.

—Jean Cocteau

The last thing I would accuse a cat of is innocence.

—Edward Palley

Never ask a hungry cat whether he loves you for yourself alone.

—Louis J. Camuti

In a cat's eye, all things belong to cats.

—English proverb

Cats can work out mathematically the exact place to sit that will cause the most inconvenience.

—Pam Brown

Cats are always elegant.

—John Weitz

You can't look at a sleeping cat and be tense.

—Jane Pauley

Those who feed cats will have sun on their wedding day.

—Welsh proverb

If there is one spot of sun spilling onto the floor, a cat will find it and soak it up.

—Joan Asper McIntosh

To assume a cat's asleep is a grave mistake. He can close his eyes and keep both his ears awake.

—Aileen Fisher

When I play with my cat, how do I know that she is not passing time with me, rather than I with her?

—Michel de Montaigne

Chapter 32

A cat can purr its way out of anything.

—*Donna McCrohan*

Happiness does not light gently on my shoulder like a butterfly. She pounces on my lap, demanding that I scratch behind her ears.

—*Author Unknown*

Cats are connoisseurs of comfort.

—*James Herriot*

The little furry buggers are just deep, deep wells you throw all your emotions into.

—*Bruce Schimmel*

When she rolls over on her back, the way horses do, only far more gracefully, a little wave peaking and curling over itself, she is the most joyful thing alive.

—*Rosellen Brown*

Cats find malicious amusement in doing what they are not wanted to do—and that with an affectation of innocence that materially aggravates their deliberate offense.

—*Helen Winslow*

Let us be honest: most of us rather like our cats to have a streak of wickedness. I should not feel quite easy in the company of any cat that walked around the house with a saintly expression.

—*Beverly Nichols*

Printed in the United States
By Bookmasters